Masculine Vulnerabilities
The POWER of an inner man revealed

HOLLIS PEARSON MEDIA
a subsidiary of

HOLLIS MEDIA GROUP

Masterful – Revealing –

Funny

ISBN 13: 978-0-692-99901-1
Library of Congress Control Number 2017963666
Copyright ©2017 by Hollis Media Group for Dunn Pearson, Jr.

This book was printed in the United States of America.

10   9   8   7   6   5   4   3   2   1

Cover: Darrell Gresham, Hollis Media Group
Editor: Katy Dawson

To order additional copies contact the Publisher:
Email: Hollismediagroup@outlook.com
Website: www.Hollismedia.net

Table of Contents

. . . the inner power of a man revealed

"A real man shows up when it matters most and knows when to bow out when it matters even more . . . We know our beginning and accept our end, but never without protest to ensure it's time to let go."

-UNKNOWN

DEDICATION

To my wonderful mother, Jewell. Thank you for the life lessons that you taught which showed me how to be a respectable man, one who works diligently and believes in the impossible to soar above the status quo. You always inspired me to give my all, and emphasized that I should never back away from a challenge, but to embrace every opportunity to flourish. Well, I took your advice again, this time not as a composer or music supervisor, but as a first-time author. I took the plunge.

My two-and-half year journey has finally come full circle; I thank God, every day that I have you with me to share the amazing journey of fulfillment.

Just getting started!!

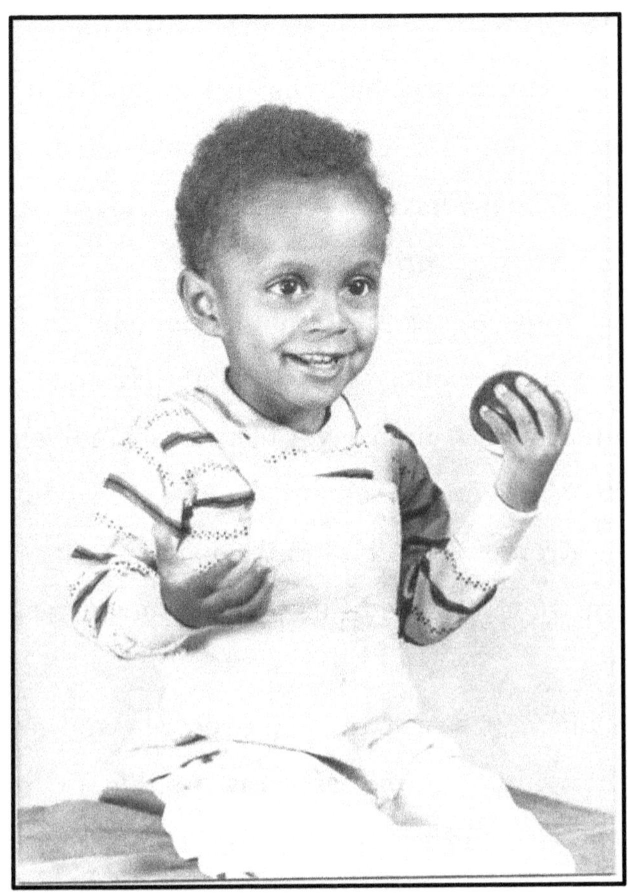

FOREWORD

I am more than pleased to talk about Donnie—that's what we call him. I've known him since he was a teenager and had the privilege of watching him grow, not just as a person, but as a talented musician; he is a prolific producer, writer, arranger, and the *consummate* musician.

Dunn joined the O'Jays as our keyboard player while in College at Kent State. Even then, he exhibited such a high level of professionalism and tenacity that I hadn't seen in a young person his age. He has strong work ethics and consumes music with such passion... in addition he is a strategic team player.

I have to say, many young people who get into the entertainment industry are unable to handle fame, access, and success. Though Dunn was thrust into the spotlight it did not alter him in a negative way. Sure, it was daunting at times, but he wasn't wild with the access. Of course, he, like all musicians had his share of ladies that hung around, that comes with the territory. But what I like about him is he never allowed any of that to impede his ability to deliver and perform his job. Dunn was accountable and trustworthy.

I really admire the guy and he is more than just a former band member, he is my friend. We talk often about our journey and he is still candid and open as ever. He's someone you can trust to tell you the truth. He always had his business intact and whatever he did, he gave it 100%. And I know this book will exhibit that same spirit of honesty and inspire thoughtful debate that will create many conversations to enlighten, inspire and challenge what we think about masculine vulnerabilities. Those who know him will not be surprised at his candid approach to a very delicate subject.

Lastly, I have the utmost respect for a young man who worked hard and determined to make something successful out of his life, and he did... when he left the O'Jays, Dunn went to New York and carved out his place in the world. I admire that.

Walter Williams, Sr.

Lead Singer, the O'Jays
Rock 'n' Roll Hall of Fame

INTRODUCTION

Masculine Vulnerabilities: Really, what is that in a man?

When I was approached by the publisher about writing a book, my thoughts of honor were foremost my emotion. The great feeling that somehow my career had been worthy of interest overwhelmed me. Then the doubts about whether I could actually write a book set in. I found it amazing at how many emotions could be felt in such a short period.

As the publisher further explained the details of the book deal, my mind wandered to what would be the subject of the book, for as a songwriter, I always began by creating the subject matter or what we called the "hook"; the line in a song that is repeated over and over again. I remembered my stage days with the "O'Jays" where we would keep "vamping" the hook to work the audience into a frenzy.

Without question, I lived the consummate bachelor's life—having access at my level has been a privilege. And many times, I expected, well, sometimes demanded more than what I was willing to give. I secretly entertained one of my concepts was going to include how I felt like a king; the women who fulfilled my every sexual fantasy, the hearts I broke, and the ones I left longing for more. Now, this made sense to me.

As an entertainer, of course, I've seen a lot of things, some of which I don't have time to talk about, and then several elements are essential to address. Although I was a little self-conscious—I am a first-time author, and the last thing I want to do is piss a lot of women off. We, men, do not like to admit it, but they are indeed a force with which to contend. At one point, I was more enraptured with talking about all the high moments, but the push-back I got from the publisher increased my angst. To my dismay, none of this was to be; we were not on the same page.

By now I have almost entirely tuned out the publisher as my perfect idea for this book has come to me. I had no title, however, I figured I would write a book like a classical composition, complete with movements (chapters) and each movement would consist of the uniqueness of my career.

My career goals and subsequent successes were that I strived to become knowledgeable and participate in most facets of the music and entertainment industry: Records, Movies, Television, Commercials, and Broadway. I am very proud that starting from playing the piano to writing for orchestras, I achieved a measure of success in each of these entertainment mediums and most importantly, I was able to earn a living doing what I loved to do. Like most boys, I was taught that you had better have a backup plan (side job); I had decided at an early age that everything I did would be music related.

I am bursting with excitement to interrupt the conversation and share my idea. However, fear of rejection and doubt that a first-time writer could have an idea so quickly has set in. So, I start to tell music industry stories in hopes that this will lead to the publisher coming around to an idea that would allow me to interject my ideas (a.k.a. fantasies) intelligently, and some realities too. I had an exciting journey and thousands of untold stories that I wouldn't mind committing to paper.

Well, this process took weeks to manifest. One day, my publisher advises that I should write a book titled Masculine Vulnerabilities. "Huh," I thought. "What in the world is that, and what does that have to do with my music success?" I listened to her explanation that after talking with me, she realized that I had lived a life that needed to speak to men about how to recognize and resolve issues of being vulnerable on all levels. While addressing men, women would get insight into the way men think; why we act as we do and certainly get some understanding of why we do the things we do. In other words, I have to get "deep" (in depth) with the readers.

Then, I was forced to deal with complexing moments that I would not have shared, but my publisher got me talking about other pertinent periods of my life; the people I've worked with, those who were favorites and what were some of the awkward moments that made me feel exposed. Another type of vulnerability spoken less about: Male-on-male vulnerability. More on these adult moments in Chapter 9.

OMG, my mind began to race, does she mean she wants me to "tell" all my friends and colleague's secrets? I cannot write a book where I would betray all trust. I would be a "snitch." I understand that scandals sometimes sell, and celebrity tales are good for business.

My mind is engaging with examples of celebrity stories; however, I now realize that many stories fit this masculine vulnerability concept. How did she know this? "Oh well, I guess that's why she's the publisher," I laugh to myself.

My publisher continues to elaborate on the aspects of storytelling, and all I can think about is how am I going to write about the world's most famous dad or my Rock-N-Roll Hall of Famers? "My Tony Award Winner would be a book in itself"; I amuse myself. The riveting behind the scenes negotiations and gossip with high profiled businesspeople could have a downright chilling effect on my career. Regarding dealing with male-on-male vulnerability, intellectually I understood this subject would be good for this book, but my stories would include one of the most prolific writers of our time including Mr. James Baldwin, also playwright for my Broadway show and a seven-time Grammy winner. I realize, "damn, I have a lot of stories!"

Now, I have thoroughly tuned out the present conversation as the "creative hook" is starting to formulate. I can write about some of my celebrity encounters not from a non-gossip perspective but my personal observation. For example, Joe Jackson  (world's famous dad) was labeled an abuser to his sons. It was ironic that in certain aspects and media situations, I found myself defending him while condemning the abuse I suffered at the hand of my then-stepfather. Alone in my thoughts, I had to reconcile this is somewhat hypocritical. Though I never endorsed his abuse, the difference was Joe, and I had a very frank discussion whereas I never gave my abuser that opportunity. In a way, Joe became the conduit for my eventual forgiveness. As a man, these are vast types of vulnerability. "Wow, I'm starting to understand my publisher"; I chuckle as I tune back in.

When I modified my vision, and expanded my approach to the book, it became apparent I had missed a lot of pertinent parts because I am now being led to deal with male vulnerability issues way beyond my initial thoughts. Though uncomfortable, I was beginning to be receptive to direction as my confidence in the "creative hook" was growing.

Well, one such complexing moment I had to recall was a vulnerability of the masculine kind—boys playing silly games: The intrigue and exploration thereof during development when young boys discover their sexuality. We play senseless games, and nothing is ever thought of it. One, in particular, men as young boys make comparison among each other about whose penis is larger and so many other assertions without any prejudice (no homophobic tendencies). And it is openly accepted as just a game that most boys play akin to girls, whom I'm told, make comparisons about the size of their breasts.

The publisher raising the bar with the vulnerability subject content forced me to think about more than originally planned. Sure, I've been hit on by a few notable male celebrities, but never discussed the approach, or by whom, and now I'm beginning to sense my publisher wants me to delve into this more. Some of the advances made toward me were a little over-the-top and I'll just stop right there for now.

In grappling with my content, and how to condense everything so that readers could have a meaningful takeaway weighed on every decision.

Thus, part of the reason this project took over two years to complete.

I laugh every time I think about this book as this realization came to me. The process by which my publisher and I approved the title for this book was filled with vulnerabilities, starting with my emotions. What I just described, coupled with the fact my publisher is a woman who used diplomacy and caution not to bruise my male "I know everything" ego. She constantly reminds me, "Dunn, I am so honored to follow your lead". To validate her wisdom in arriving at this title, my response is "Yea, we men think we are leading when actually we know we are being led." This was no different.

I am happy that I still get to write my classical composition. Though, I will reveal the inner thoughts of creating the score (chapters), while hopefully at the end, I have created a masterpiece that sounds good or in the literary world "a work of substance," to provoke thought and is entertaining.

Okay, let me digest the "hook" Masculine Vulnerabilities.

Before I look up the definitions of these two powerful words, I offer my first impression.

Being born a man doesn't automatically make you masculine. That is a learned trait... Depending on the teacher, the amount of masculine behavior will vary. That variance will impact every decision a man makes throughout life. These decisions become the agent of change. The degree of change will be based on the negative or positive outcomes.

It is very rare that any other influence will consciously change a man's masculine trait. Growing from a child to a man, he becomes physically and mentally stronger as does his masculine personality. He finds products of living to enhance his masculine lifestyle. From fast cars to exotic women, he sees these as toys of definitions. However, subconsciously these toys become defining vulnerable agents that could leave a man questioning his very existence.

Being true to my own vulnerabilities, I will not reveal all my personal teachers, as you will draw conclusions about the merits of the teachings. Thus, I hope my candid revelations will inspire you to read my next book titled "Something About the Hour" in which I will reveal how I evaluate my childhood teachings relating to my adult life.

Now to the dictionary...

Masculinity is a set of traits, attributes, behaviors, and roles generally associated with boys and men. Traits traditionally cited include courage, independence, and assertiveness.

Vulnerabilities are circumstances where one could be easily harmed physically, mentally, and emotionally.

With this understanding, I surmise it must have been the music story about how every girl in the audience wanted to be with me is how my publisher derived from this subject.

When I questioned why this title, she indicated this is what she heard. That I lived vulnerably (emotionally unprotected) that resonated – since I was always putting myself in a relationship that forced me to unveil despite my trying to conceal real emotions.

Wow! I didn't realize she was listening to me that intently, but I guess this is what I am supposed to share with the world.

The man and his music... now the path forward as a literary genius.

CHAPTER 1
The
DICHOTOMY

As an entertainer, it would be easy for me to excuse so many of my actions because having RANDOM flings, access to various *taboos* and privilege come with the territory. Though, most entertainers, embody the worst ideology—that we are entitled. A perspective of one's value and importance to the world that could lead to many poor life choices. Of course, the sentiment is magnified a thousand times stronger if you are a male entertainer because most people (*women*) never say "**no**" to you, which isn't a good thing.

It creates a vacuum whereby excess becomes the drug that we pump into our veins that lead to intoxication from the applause and *convoluted* affection showered upon us; in addition, the idea that other people think we are somehow different and very special apart from them—Aristocrats if you will, only adds to the emotional frenzy of mixed emotions, and misguided decisions we make. Sometimes we don't know what people want from us; male or female. The time allotted to figure it out where people are coming from, occasionally diminishes the best intentions we have at the onset.

However, what my consciousness gifted me is a sense of understanding—as a man, my realization is I have a unique place in the world, and responsibility to make a difference no matter what level of privilege I enjoy. The other awareness is as a man, I, as most men, expend too much energy creating false-positives whereby we lie to ourselves that we can handle everything because nothing bothers us. After all, we are men. In reality, we need to be reassured, nurtured, understood, and allotted space to be who we are deep down inside: Rumbustious little boys. That is why we sometimes continue to do silly things even though most women think our adolescence is a thing of the past. Wrong.

We adapt very easily to create and find new toys to play with . . . Sometimes what we indulge in will only make sense to another man. Occasionally, it is truly a man-thing. Sadly, the manner in which we go about this is from time-to-time, so out of sync with the established tenor in an existing relationship; our communication skills or lack thereof, often gets us in trouble and exasperates our partner.

Primarily, it is this hidden, unspoken aspect of who we really are that creates a vacuum; we sometimes induce a feeling that makes a woman feel unappreciated and under-valued. Though, for most men who are genuinely sincerely about their relationship, this is not the outcome we had in mind.

Somewhere we get off track and out of alignment, and the longer the missteps persist, it takes twice as long for us to realign. The other negative characteristic of this is, we misinterpret the tolerance level of women as *"approval."* When you 'FAKE' everything is cool, you are yet building upon that glass house, which eventually comes crashing down.

For *"**some**"* women, their first position is to cry foul; however, you need to understand and accept your contribution that built this unsustainable dwelling too...A healthy relationship can only exist and thrive where there is honesty. You can't hide and pretend when shit is falling apart just because you don't want to be alone. You too, have to deal with it. To step up emotionally and cease muddying up the waters.

Notwithstanding, our falling short in communicating, and in other behavioral situations should not be misconstrued; we do man-up and take care of business. However, what I am indicating is men have multiple personality traits, and one that is often rejected is our boyhood tendencies just because we are a man. Those of us, who love women, go through several phases of trying to have as many of them as we can – it's crazy but true. It is this type of *irrational unsustainable access* many view as a calling card that signifies to the world we are "really" somebody, and because of it, will discount how we handle women. Sadly, often damaging the one who has been our bedrock through all types of fluctuations. We fuck up.

We, men, are also scared of some women who are passive-aggressive; those who fake being timid, but as we spend more time with them, we see are vicious barracudas and will place them in a category. We may continue to engage in sex for a period of time, but will also go to the extreme not to commit emotionally. Men are masters at compartmentalizing our interaction to extract only what we need and will not invest any more than necessary to obtain what we want. It's the function within dysfunction.

Our personal conflict is intertwined with the need to belong and to be important to somebody; to have something exclusive that gives us bragging rights because we love to talk and hype up things. I think all men are salesmen; some, are more polished than others but never think we don't embellish—it is in our DNA, and it starts very early.

This is why young boys have been known to put socks within their pants to give the illusion of their anatomy being larger than what it is; we are wired to dominate and inflate. Our actions are often akin to the COBRA that must raise its hood to give the appearance, it is bad. What most men are too afraid to tell you is "WE ARE ALSO INSECURE." And are gun-shy at the slightest deviation from our constructed image of ourselves if we have not spent time to learn who we are individually, and this is reflected in all types of relationships.

Unfortunately, we often cause more harm than good because a man who doesn't know he is SELFISH, will never consider what a woman needs or wants from him because he only sees his needs and everything else is secondary. He is a man without balance and strives to attain more of what brings the greatest pleasure, coupled with allowances to be, and do whatever he chooses without consequence. Having his cake and eating it too.

Life presents to us numerous options by which we are confronted with many narratives from which to choose, but here are two distinct ones: 1) Those who live lawlessly and overlook all universal principles by which humanity is governed will not escape the boomerang of their deeds or 2) As freewill-agents, men will eventually evolve where one's lifestyle will reflect the mantra "I Shall Do No Harm" and live a kick-ass life here on earth.

Our intricacy is what some women find alluring; the mystique that some men exhibit can be a powerful aphrodisiac – the warrior, lover, friend, protector, and provider. In summation, no matter what personality traits we display, at the end of the day we just want to mean something, and we don't like SHARING what we deem exclusive with anybody.

GETTING STARTED!

CHAPTER 2
NOT THERE YET

Men basically teach boys to "man-up." Be strong, never show signs of weakness, handle your business, and just have no fear. Women teach boys the difference between right and wrong. They instill a sense of pride in standing up for our beliefs and taking the proper actions in the face of adversity. To embrace *spirituality*, which is also enforced in connection with the church. That belief in a higher power regardless of religion gives boys an inner strength. Though these are generalities and teachings may be interchangeable, parents, family, friends, peers, idols, and heroes administer most teachings.

I want to now share many of my life's Masculine Vulnerabilities.

In elementary school, boys hung with the boys and girls did whatever they did with the girls. We acted silly in class to get a laugh, talked loudly and generally didn't pay attention to the teacher. Back in the day, the teacher would give you a paddle if you got out of line and my 4th-grade teacher was no exception. Her method of punishment would make the student gather rulers from fellow students and then use that newly formed weapon on your hands. It was the same as mothers making you go outside and get a switch from a bush. I would watch as the "bad boys" would weep as this teacher would wail on their hand. Of course, after school, we would tease the bad boy by calling him a girl. I did everything I could not to get paddled.

However, I knew deep down I wanted to see if I could take the pain and of course, I had to prove I was a man. So, one day my turn came to collect the rulers. Unfortunately for me, my teacher recognized my little plan and was not going to stop until I was crying. I tried so hard not to cry, but in the end, that paddle hurt.

The aftermath was expected with the teasing yet, what was unexpected, a girl told me she liked me. After thinking how nasty that sounded to me over the next months I couldn't help myself, I liked her too.

During this time, the school band teacher had chosen me to play trombone in the school band. I found that odd because I had been taking piano lessons about two years though I didn't tell anyone. What I thought was odd was that he didn't ask me if I played any instrument, he simply chose me to play trombone because the band didn't have anyone else to play trombone.

Springtime brought about the band performance for the school, and because of my hidden piano and music reading skills, I was chosen to perform a trombone solo. I was so excited, yet scared and embarrassed to play in front of all my schoolmates when it was my turn to walk onto the stage.

Suddenly, I hear all this laughter as I keep playing. I am thinking that they are just being fools only to see my teacher standing in the wings as I come offstage. She calmly reaches down and zips my pants. Now I know why the laughter was so loud. As my eyes well up with tears, again this girl I like approaches and comfort me. She tells me I played well, never mentions my fly being open. Now I am in love.

Now even though I didn't like the teasing, it didn't seem to bother me as much because I had my girl. I must tell her she is my official girl which at one time would have an impossible step to take. What do I say? Saying anything was out of the question, I could never get any words out like that. Kiss her? Nope, too nasty. I got it; I'll write a love letter. It took days, probably weeks to finally write these words; I remember, "I need you like grass needs water." Wow! That was masterful!! I was too shy to give it to her face-to-face, so I left it on her desk.

After band class, I stood nervously as I knew I would see her as usual. She would always look good and had a beautiful grin on her face and had a laugh I could hear a mile away. She lived in my neighborhood, and her younger brother hung out with my group of friends. He looked up to me, and I had a sense of hidden pride when her parents would thank me for looking out for him. They would feed me as all mothers in the neighborhood tended to do. Though her parents would joke that one day their daughter and I would get married, I never let on that I hoped that too.

All these emotions came full circle as she approached me, telling me she read the letter. Without saying a word, she grabbed my hand and pulled me behind the stage curtain and kissed me on my lips. This wasn't nasty, quite the opposite; she had a taste and smell that if I think hard enough, I can still recollect this day some 40 years later. Needless to say, I am sitting on top of the world.

I cannot remember what I did in the afternoon class; I would not have cared if got paddled, teased, or beat up in a fight. All I could think about was that kiss and when I might get another one. Ah, I would get that chance a little later before leaving school as we would go to the music room to gather our instruments to take home.

Though I couldn't wait to get to the music room, I purposely fooled around with the boys, so I wouldn't seem too excited. As I walked around the stage curtain, I see my girl kissing another boy. Well, what happened next was typical, she looked at me with that oops, I'm sorry look, but oh well. I cried all the way home and sooner or later the boy, and I got into a fight. Of course, the fight was about something that had nothing to do with the girl.

Masculine Vulnerabilities.

Sometimes, unforeseen change will force you in the right direction.

CHAPTER 3
FORCED OUT

Years have passed, and now I have reached Junior High School. I should be happy because of my "smartness"; I was chosen to go to a special school for student enrichment. However, I am not happy because the school my mother selected for me is far away from the neighbor, and the school district where I lived had just built a brand-new school within walking distance from my home. Most of my friends are attending there, and I could not understand why my mother chose to send me across town. Though, my mother enrolled me in a different district, which meant I had to travel either by city bus or walk. The bus trip would take about an hour, and the walk was at least 10-15 miles.

My mother had this brainy idea to enroll me in this school for enrichment; somehow this was supposed to be good for me. It didn't make sense, nor did I care to share her enthusiasm for starting over in a new learning environment. I was thrust out my comfort zone and probably would not have protested as much if the change wasn't so drastic. It'll become clearer what I mean by this.

The first day of school was filled with the normal awkwardness; however, it was also permeated with amplified anxiety as I realize this school was not in a great neighborhood. Some would call this the hood. I thought I was attending a school for smart people. Now I am getting the meaning of some of my early teachings that there are two types of smart; street smart and book smart. I realize that these two kinds of people are probably not going to mix well together because the looks I am getting from the street-smart are threatening.

The bright spot of this day was that a girl named Jackie was also attending. This girl was a cousin to one of my neighborhood friends whom during a family visit I fell in "like." The word like was the "chosen pet" word of the times as love was out of the question. From the first moment I saw her, I knew I had to get this exotic girl to like me. She carried herself differently from any other girl I knew. She had a beautiful smile and lips I couldn't wait to kiss.

I pestered my friend for her phone number but never succeeded, so my prior contact had been limited to seeing her on family visits. During these family visits, she barely paid me any attention and this first day of school was only slightly different in the fact that she acknowledged knowing me by saying hello. Nonetheless, she gave me a reason to look forward to attending this school.

My worst fears came true as the name calling "smarty pants," "nerds" and "wimps" were echoed through the halls as we, the smart ones, would walk to class together. There was a slight comfort in being together for classes; however, we were integrated into the total school community during homeroom period. Homeroom was a student's first class. It has been to me just a place where the teacher would take attendance, and we would put our belongings in our locker, and get our books for the next class. I hated coming to homeroom because of a guy named Richard.

He had a habit of finger thumping everyone on the head. Thump, thump, thump he would march down the aisle. The teacher seemed never to punish him. The mode of punishment in this school was the teacher would send you to the gym teacher who had an inch-thick wooden paddle.

Depending on the degree of violation, the student would receive a number of swats. The student would be taken to a stairwell and had to bend over holding the step while being swatted.

The reverberation of that sound could be heard throughout the entire floor. Adding the howl of the student made for a very frightening deterrent. Needless to say, we could not wait for Richard to get paddled; however, that day never seemed to come.

To make matters worse, on the stairwell to the cafeteria there was a group of bullies who gathered daily. Their ringleader would approach and demand my lunch money to pass. This was more intense than the homeroom thumper because it involved taking my pride, manhood, and choice to eat lunch. They were taking my parents' money with the threat that I better not tell anyone. I tried to avoid them by trying to sneak around someone else while they were collecting some other boy's money. I would hide my money in my shoe, but none of these techniques worked, the ringleader seemed to be incredibly street smart, and I couldn't figure out any book-smart way to stop him.

Well, like a Hollywood script, it happened. You guessed it, the bully took my lunch money, and I believe Jackie saw it though she never said anything. The breaking point was reached. That night it was impossible to sleep; I couldn't think of anything except what I was going to do all night. My anticipation of going to school the next day was at an all-time high. I remember waking the following day, coming back to the reality that I wasn't going to do nothing except give him my money.

However, a domestic event at my home earlier that morning caused me to be in a very bad mood.

All fear vanished... I wasn't in the mood for nobody's bullshit.

I was (am) a spoiled only child. I was used to getting and having my way about everything. My parents divorced, and my mom remarried. My then stepfather had just recently moved his nephew, named Benny in with us and in a sense, I had a brother. Benny and I went through all the sharing adjustments and growing pains. Looking back, our family issue was simple at its core; Benny and my stepfather were street-smart and my mother (also an only child and participated in several special major work school programs) and I, were very book smart.

When I got to homeroom, I wasn't thinking about anything or anybody. My mind was just filled with frustration. My mind had finally wandered to Jackie, and suddenly, I felt the dreaded thump on my head. Before I knew it, I had picked Richard up into the air and flung him against the lockers. As he lay on the floor, I kicked him repeatedly in the face. The amazing thing was that my classmates were cheering me on. No one came to break up this one-sided fight that went on for what seemed to be an eternity. When I awakened from what I would later describe as a "blackout" . . . My teacher had a look of foolish surprise that I was capable of such a violent act as this. I was given no punishment.

Keeping to the Hollywood script, when lunchtime came around, my confrontation with the bullies was anti-climactic. I looked at the ringleader, and he merely backed off never again to take my money. I don't know if he had heard about my morning exploits, but there was never another day where myself or anyone that was with me, would ever be threatened or robbed. End of the story. The fighter within my soul was unleashed; no longer tethered to fear and to my surprise, so was my courage to confront difficulty.

I guess you are wondering where the masculine vulnerability is in this chapter. My eyes are beginning to well up with tears as I am writing the actual truth to this story. Every detail is correct on the surface, however, during my entire life when telling this story, I have omitted these truths: I didn't blackout in my fight with Richard, in fact, I remember every detail, every punch and kick. It was not the teacher that stopped me from continuing; it was the look of terror and pure fright in Richard's eyes. He and I knew I could have killed him with my bare hands. I was ready to kill him, and he was literally begging and pleading for me not just to stop beating him, but for his life. I was sick to my stomach that my inner rage had come to the surface. I was now what I had vowed never to be, a street-smart thug.

When I got near the bully, my inner personality was on full display. I looked him in the eye with a look that said to him, "Motherfucker, if you ever as so much as look at me without a smile on your face I will throw your stupid ass down these damn steps."

I remember he looked down the steps and without us exchanging a single word, his street smarts told him of how vulnerable he was in trying to rob someone standing in a stairwell. The truth is I was never scared to have been beaten by his hands. Masculine Vulnerabilities. The reality at that moment was, I was already dealing with that type of threat at home by my then *stupid-ass* abusive stepfather.

One more admission before I move on to the next chapter. I couldn't resist getting the feel of that paddle. It hurt!

*Everything **EVENTUALLY** comes full circle.*

CHAPTER 4
BACK HOME

High school was great. I was back to the neighborhood school with all my friends, and Jackie finally liked me. The time I invested in this relationship was well worth it. My boys didn't have a reason to tease me anymore; actually, they were jealous I had a girlfriend and Life was looking up. My real dad really liked Jackie as well and would let me drive his car on dates with her. Most importantly, my mom approved, granting permission to see Jackie whenever possible. I guess we were in "puppy love." Though this puppy love was teenagers experimenting with love, this relationship turned out to be one of the most important in my growth as a man.

The result of the long time it took Jackie to like me was not just the dedication I had for her, my emotions had time to develop. What Jackie gave me in return would be the number one quality I would find myself looking for in every girl for the rest of my life. Her gift to me was unconditional trust. All men are raised and teased that we are looking for a mate like their mother. It took me a long time to fully understand that—what it really meant was that we are looking for someone that we can love the way we love our mother (unconditionally). Mama jokes were cause for immediate fights.

Unconditional love for mom is standard. These traits are embedded in most men. A mother's love provides inner strength that most men didn't know they possess and I was no exception. When I would experience moments of masculine vulnerability, the thought of showing that perceived weakness to my mom encouraged to get me through the situation.

Competing with a mother's love is virtually impossible, especially as a girlfriend. However, Jackie proved to be close, because her unconditional trust provided me the emotional security to freely experiment with life.

My school had a huge entertainment show approaching; the high school talent show was the number one entertainment show of the entire school year. Benny Slocum (drums) and I had formed a band with Kenny Redon (Guitar) and Ernie Cary (Bass), later adding Bobby English (Sax) and Conga Redd named "The Shades of Soul" and the anticipation was sky high. Filled with angst, I couldn't sleep the night before, so I went down to the basement to do a private practice. "Sly & Family Stone" was my favorite group so of course, I was going to imitate *"Sly"* complete with outfit. His album featured him with a knitted cap and big fur boots. My mom took me all over town searching for fur boots. Finally, we found my fur boots at a ski shop. Wow, my emotions are beyond raising the roof, hell, I could raise the whole house.

It is close to showtime and jitters set in. My hands are sweating—I paced back and forth. Suddenly, calm was restored, and as that peace took over, I realized that no matter what happens Jackie would be there for me. We opened our set with Sly's song "I Wanna Thank You For Lettin' Me Be Myself". The band started playing first to allow for my grand entrance. I simply walked to center stage and opened my arms. My fellow students went crazy with applause. I went to the organ and proceeded to play with one arm behind my back. To cap it off, I imitated Jimi Hendrix by playing the organ with my nose and mouth. To this day my classmates have used social media to remind me of this memory. After this night, I was a high school star.

Jackie's unconditional trust would be tested in the days to come. I tried to stay level-headed, but that was hard considering my head wouldn't fit through the school door. Some upper-class girls took notice of me, but I was too shy for any immediate interaction. My self-confidence or lack thereof limited my action to mere nervous smiling.

Then I met Ruby, a girl that was visiting friends in my neighborhood. Ruby lived in my grandmother's neighborhood, so I thought *okay* "**no one** would know." We exchanged phone numbers and started long telephone conversations. This time was the pre-cell phone era, so the phone I would learn would become the real mode of getting to know someone.

However, my male machismo would be not to waste time talking and spend time with action if you know what I mean. So, Ruby and I were to meet again at a church dance. I had all these plans of dancing and then going outside for some real fun. Not only did I not dance with her, but we also didn't say one word to each other. I barely looked at her, and she probably didn't look at me either. The reason this event has always stuck with me is that the irony is that as soon as I got home, I telephoned her and resumed conversation as if the dance never happened.

It took years before I understood it was my allegiance to Jackie that played the major part of why no words or actions came that dance night.

Additionally, it was Jackie's trust that allowed me to share my inner thoughts with Ruby knowing that my risk of emotional vulnerability was limited. Make no mistake, Ruby and I shared all our vulnerable emotions during these long telephone conversations.

. . . life had moved forward—

You see Jackie trusted that no matter what I did (big head) —I would come home to her. This trust would become a trait I'd desire and exhibit throughout the rest of my journey. My regret is that the lack of understanding of how to properly use this trust cost me, Jackie. As I eventually tried a relationship with an upper classmate. By the time I realized the importance of that trust trait to my growth in manhood, life had moved forward — Masculine Vulnerabilities.

According to my publisher, I am to offer teachable moments in my writing. That my experiences could inspire conscious examination of how male-female relationships can be healthier, sexier, and happier, or, couples would remain wild and free. Regardless if one is dating or married, there is something to garner--all aspect of my journey is a vital lesson. If a woman can truly exhibit unconditional trust, she will gain as I have shown a lifetime friend whom can be counted and depended upon at any times of need. You will gain "my folks" status for life, which means you will be considered family, regardless the outcome of the relationship. It won't matter whether either party has a new mate, you will never lose your status. The exchange will always be a platform of truth - real candid, any answers you need to conundrums when truly desired.

---

*Men definitely see life through
a different prism.*

I remember actually apologizing to one of "my folks"-- although I hadn't been with her in many years when my jealousy was clouding my advice to her on how to handle a situation with a new man in her life. She has thanked me throughout life as my candid advice has paid off for both her career and private life. However, men will test that trust because it is so connected to our emotional vulnerability. We feel that if we totally put our "mother's love" into a woman, our ego and control would be at risk.

The violation should the woman be perceived as faking this trust will lead to stalking, domestic violence, and crazy cheating.

Speaking of cheating, as bizarre as this may sound, a man will use trust as a license to experiment. In our sub-conscious mind, we are trying to perfect our techniques and show emotions with no emotional risk because we have "our folks" at home. This is why women get such adamant confessions of innocence when confronted. We truly don't perceive that having an affair as cheating because you are "folks"; the other person is just temporary fun or sowing of oats. We actually surmise that we are cheating to make our relationship with you better.

However, don't get it twisted, in a man's mind you are not allowed to do the same thing unless the guy is providing you unconditional trust. As difficult as it is to receive and properly honor such trust, it is equally as difficult to give such trust. I have done that all of two times in years, and sometimes shudder to think why only twice because the results have been so rewarding. Masculine Vulnerabilities.

GROUPIES-WHO KNEW THERE WAS MORE?

CHAPTER 5

1ˢᵗ *Road Trip* –
Introduction to Groupies

Anticipation, anxiety, and excitement, filled the air as we loaded all the equipment into the truck. This fall night in 1971 was our first road trip to Philadelphia for a 3-night weekend performance engagement. We were bursting with so many emotions that we didn't even mind the fact that the manager had taken a couch from the office and put it in the back of a windowless U-Haul truck—we sat in the dark the entire trip. After all, we were teenagers between 13 and 17 yrs. Old and we didn't care.

Our group, the "Shades of Soul," was the backup band for the singing group the "Ponderosa Twins" whose hit record "You Send Me" was blazing up the charts. The group was marketed and promoted in the style of another hot and upcoming act like the "Jackson Five."

Though the "Ponderosa Twins" were not a total family group. They consisted of two sets of identical twins and a little lead singer who sounded very similar to Michael Jackson. The group's producer was founding member of the "O'Jays," Bobby Massey, who taught us everything we needed to know about performing. He was very demanding, and a taskmaster as his number one rule was "practice." We rehearsed daily for 8-10 hours. I was married to the music-- interwoven into my spirit, I could play the songs in my sleep.

As our caravan of cars and truck left the city limits of Cleveland, I remember feeling a sense of independence. No parents, no rules, or curfews coupled with sharing this moment with all of my bandmates—I felt no longer as a kid but a man. There were the usual wisecracks, idle chatter and verbally ripping up each other. However, when it came to the subject of girls, there seemed to be a drop-off in the usual bravado about how many girls we were going to have—the realization of actually doing it was about to come.

My mind quickly drifted back to my duties as piano player and bandleader. I was confident that I would play the music correctly, relying on my previous success from performing in talent shows. I was looking forward to the audience's reaction. My only concern was how our talents would match up against the other acts on the show. Well, it seemed that before I could answer these questions in my mind, we were arriving at the hotel.

Money didn't matter; we were aiming for stardom . . . We were paid a whopping $5 per Diem and didn't complain.

The next morning, I was quickly reminded that I wasn't a man as our support personnel awakened us with rules; show schedules and most importantly the $5.00 Per diem. As we pulled up to the Uptown Theater in Philadelphia, the marque had our name along with the "Main Ingredient"; "New Birth"; "Nite-Lighters" and, "Brenda and The Tabulations." Now I am feeling some nervousness, but never admit this to anyone.

The show schedule was grueling. It was like a movie schedule: five shows a day--12 pm, 3 pm, 6 pm, 9 pm and a 12:00 Midnight show. Oh well, once again we didn't care. We even overlooked the whopping $10.00 per show salary.

All the performing acts quickly arrived, and I again felt like a kid as all the other performers appeared much older and more seasoned. I found myself trying to mimic what others were doing such as hanging backstage, testing the equipment, and going out the stage door as if checking the guests arriving when they were interested to see if anybody noticed who they were.

Suddenly a loud voice rang out "HALF HOUR!" This would become a consistent sound as the stage manager is announcing that there was a half hour before Showtime. At this moment, my nerves and eagerness to get rolling are reaching high notes.

Our first performance seemed like a blur as I know we played it, but my mind only recalls the first screams from the sold-out crowd of what appeared to me all young girls. From there all I heard was more screaming and more applause. Now my mind is focused on the reality of all my dreams of adoring fans, girls, music, girls, and more music.

After the show, the majority of performers went to their dressing room to change clothes and then hung out outside the stage door to greet fans and sign autographs. Well, that didn't seem like a good strategy for me because they were older and knew what to say and how to act. I was still too hyped up from the show, and I wanted to go out in the lobby where I hoped the girls would approach me.

So, I didn't change clothes; I put a towel around my neck like a prizefighter just finishing a 15-round boxing match. Scared that I would be embarrassed, I told my group I was so hungry and had to get something from the concession stand, and would be right back knowing they weren't going to spend their money.

Well, as soon as I approached the concession stand, a girl snatched the towel from around my neck as a souvenir and a mob of girls quickly multiplied. I am now in a term I would learn later as "groupie" heaven. However, as more girls crowded me something out of a classic movie happened; I noticed a pretty and appealing waitress behind the concession stand. The uproar and squealing from the girls around me somehow were canceled out in my mind. It didn't matter what they were trying to tell me; I couldn't hear them. My mind was somewhere else.

The longer I observed, I am mesmerized by the waitress' looks and fixated on her lips. I wanted to grab and kiss her. Although, I am experiencing what I always dreamt up; adorning fans who appreciated my musicianship and me, so I presumed. However, far from it. I am surrounded by girls who I later discovered were ready and willing to do a lot more than give a kiss, but I only want the attention of someone who is not paying any attention at all.

Love Struck!

I make my way to the concession stand and go out of my way to highlight the fact that I am the entertainer who is commanding all this attention and placed an order with this girl. She smiles, and promptly fills my order and gives me a look that ultimately leaves me speechless: "I know what you are doing, I see this all the time." I shyly walk away without saying a word.

The ride to the hotel was filled with macho bravado and details of the day's missions and conquests. Mine was filled with the longing for the waitress because, throughout the five (5) show intermissions, I had only made minimal progress. Well, off to bed as I was exhausted and eager to start the next day of shows—filled with expectancy in hopes of seeing that one special lady and getting closer than the day before.

Feeling invincible ...

The second show day was very similar to the first. Our show was getting very polished and tight; we were feeling invincible as the other performers were beginning to take notice of us and, were very complimentary. Our group collectively was building confidence, and our strong bond was showing in our performance.

We were very observant of the other performers, and our band was incorporating some of their music techniques exhibited. Now we were also focusing on the offstage techniques—I watched how the men handle the fans and how they spoke to the women. I began to recognize how they selectively chose women. I learned how to impress the girls while remaining humble and shy discreetly. Privately, some girls turned me on—I wanted to pounce. However, it was more imperative to stay calm—to appear desirable yet, emotionally unavailable.

I had decided that I would stay away from the waitress today so that I wouldn't seem too aggressive. The last thing I wanted her to think was that I was like every other performer that was probably all over her.

However, that was my head thoughts. My heart couldn't wait to find an excuse to go back to the concession stand. After the third show, my heart won out as I convinced myself I was extremely hungry this time. As I approached the waitress, I noticed something different about her, but I couldn't quite figure out what it was. In hindsight, it was that she had put on some makeup, which gave her an extra glow. Though she didn't say anything, she gave me an inviting smile that told me she was just as glad to see me as I was to see her.

We made small talk, and as I turned to walk away, she invited me to come back after the next show to spend the break time with her. That was probably the best show I played; I hurried to her because I wanted her to witness the groupies after me, and then I could resist them and choose her. She pretended not to notice the other girls, or maybe, she was swamped working, whichever, she smiled when I approached the counter.

This time she came from behind the counter and now I could see her entire body. I could fantasize her in my arms; though, I was still most attracted to her lips and my desire to kiss her increased. After all the techniques I just learned as to how to talk to girls, I couldn't seem to get out any of the words I wanted to say. Instead, all I could muster was idle small talk.

However, the small talk helped me learn that she, too, was in high school and her parents allowed her to work to not only make some spending money but, to keep her busy and out of trouble. I remember she was interested in becoming a writer and she was excited about talking to many entertainers to gain knowledge.

INTIMIDATING . . .

Knowing this about her was good, but also intimidating because I immediately felt like I was in competition. So, I considered my best chance was not to inflate my experience, but be honest and tell her this was my first time doing a roadshow. It proved to be good because it broke the ice and by the next break, we were having more relaxed conversations.

Though our conversations were more as platonic friends rather than boyfriend-girlfriend, I was just happy to have someone I could in my mind call "my girl."

Now my fellow bandmates had caught on to my love interest and the wisecracks were starting to mount. "My, who do you have?" was repeated numerous times by several of them. When I returned to the guys, I was met with stories of how many groupies they had, the kisses and sexual activities they were having that I was not. To prove to me that I was missing out, they invited me to a fellow member's room. As another band member and I approached the room, we could hear a lot of noise.

As we entered the room, there were two girls each lying in one of the double beds having sex with anyone that wanted to; I learned that this was called an orgy. Wow, I thought this looks like fun but disgusting. Everybody is sharing the same body sweat—nobody stopped to wash. Count me out. Plus, I was too scared to participate because my stepfather had threatened that if I got anybody pregnant, I would have to move out and become a man. I certainly wasn't going to risk that for these girls; I don't even know their name. What it did show me was that these girls at the show were willing to have sex with me. My mistake was believing the reason was that I was so great of an entertainer.

My curiosity was peaked. So why am I chasing a waitress that was like the girls back home in my high school that I dated which seem to take almost a year, and a sit down with her parents to even get a kiss and some rolling around on the couch?

Mixed emotions . . . The third and final day was filled with mixed emotions; sad to leave, glad to be heading home. Couldn't wait to brag to all the kids at school on Monday.

My anticipation to see my girl was filled with plans of professing my desire to see her again and keeping in touch. It seemed like the audiences sensed our desire to make these last shows special too. They were equally appreciative of the energy we brought to the stage. It was a true synergistic moment—everything seemed to click.

It was my last day in Philadelphia; I didn't pretend to need to go to the concession stand, and my girl didn't pretend not to notice all the attention I received from the groupies. On this day, I observed my girl had on her Sunday clothes underneath her work attire that I felt was for me. This day was different; it was special. Absent was the usual awkwardness, we were laughing and joking about everything and everybody.

After the last show, I had to pack my equipment, so I knew I wouldn't have a lot of time to say goodbye, but I hurried as fast as I could to get to the lobby. This time I didn't care about any fan or groupie; I just went straight to my girl. She was waiting patiently, and I could tell she was sad to say goodbye. As I said all the right things about wanting to stay in touch, it happened . . . My masculine vulnerabilities would now be tested.

She stopped me mid-sentence and dragged me into a closet. Now we're in a secluded place with no lights, and she put those lips I had been dreaming about on mine. It seems like this moment would last forever. Then she stuck her tongue down my throat; I am getting hot and aroused. My being euphoric and *feeling* in love with my girl I fast forward to building a lifetime relationship with someone I don't even know; it's crazy how your emotions will convince you to believe something other than the truth when you want to escape and experience something new.

I entertained spending years with this girl, though I had only known her for three whole days. Thoughts rushed through my mind about all the wonderful phone calls we are going to share. She would meet my parents, and I would meet her family. Of course, I would be a big shot because I would have an out of town girlfriend. Somehow, she would be much different and more special than the girls back home.

Then she moves her body close to mine and sticks her leg around the back of my legs, and presses her vagina area to my crouch. Oh my, oh my!

Then it HAPPENED!

Then IT HAPPENED—She reaches down and grabs my penis right through my pants. Embarrassed by how hard my penis was, I attempted to move her hand, but I didn't want to remove her hand. Her sensitive touch is causing me to lose control. Abruptly, a series of disturbing questions bombarded my mind: How is this happening? When I leave, and the next entertainer shows up, would she be unfaithful and pull him into a dark closet and rub his penis too? I am supposed to be the star here who is completely controlling this event; she should have submitted and waited for my command, but her aggressive posture stirred many conflicting emotions . . . I don't know if relationships are supposed to move this fast.

Eventually, I settled that just maybe there was something out of sync with the way I perceived how we would depart. I questioned, "Am I mad because she is destroying my rehearsed love ending; while questioning, why am I so glad she pulled me in this closet?"

Finally, I do move her hand, but as I do so, I ejaculate. As my semen is rolling down my pant leg I am thinking, is this my girl or, is she just another groupie? Am I disgusted or in love? Masculine Vulnerabilities.

There is no place like COLLEGE!!

CHAPTER 6
The Collegiate Whirlwind

College days are here, and right away I'm not loving what would turn out to be the biggest blessing of all; 7:45 AM class every morning. I thought going to college meant pretending to be an adult while on the parent's dime. Late night partying, girls, more girls, and no responsibility. I woke up every morning dreaming I was still asleep with girls, girls and well, girls. The only saving grace was that the early class was directly associated with my music composition major—music theory.

During my senior high school year, I was president of the marching band and had written the music for all the instruments by ear. In other words, I wrote the notes on the blackboard for the different instruments and hummed the melody to the musicians. I learned that this technique was used by many artists that had no formal training in music. To my surprise, what I learned in music theory was that my self-taught techniques were actually correct. My professor, Dr. Watson (also assigned as my College Advisor) provided affirmation and proper musical technique training that enhanced my skillset and expanded my terminology of what I already knew. So, every morning I began to look forward to getting up and going to class. Whatever doubts and anxiety I had faded. I gained confidence that I could flourish in college and pass this test of experimental manhood. I achieved and reached bigger horizons through a simple academic exchange—a total stranger recognizing my talent changed the perception I had of myself. A person with superior knowledge validated me. That endorsement transferred over to other critical areas of my life, and yes, my ego swelled, but I could at least back it up because I was officially talented.

Equally as important going to that early class helped in all my other classes because I attended every day. Hell, I was already up. That led to my making Dean's list, which proved to be the biggest blessing as my most challenging college economic challenge was yet to come.

Socially, I entered college vulnerable. The new experience of being surrounded by a white majority of students was a little unsettling; growing up we were always separated by racial divides in Ohio, like in most cities during this time in the 60s. I could count on one hand the number of white students that had previously been in all my classes combined. Now for the first time, I am experiencing being a minority. Sure, I had been taught the social issues of prejudice and slavery, but now it is right in front of me. My defenses were raised as I was facing the unexpected, however, the college experience was entirely different than society's projections. Quite the opposite or shall I say confusing because there was 'no in your face prejudice'; the unambiguous bullshit.

All the teachers and students treated me normal (in other words, with respect). Always helpful and open to communication. Unfortunately, the times kept us socially segregated as we had organizations such as Black United Students that informed us of instances of institutional racism. The 70s was the civil rights days, and many speakers such as Angela Davis, Rev. Ralph Abernathy and Jane Fonda came to speak. Of course, every May 4th our campus honored those protesters that lost their lives when the National Guard opened fire against students at Kent State.

During my freshman year, the Isley Brother's came to campus to perform their song "4 Dead In Ohio," and my band was chosen as the opening act. We hadn't felt this type of celebrity since the Ponderosa Twins days, and I was very excited yet nervous. This performance would be in front of upper classmates and making an impression or as I call building my image, was very important to me.

Our experience showed that night as our band rose to the occasion and the audience displayed support. As the applause grew my confidence as a college student inflated too--my classmates took stock of my talent, and nothing could make me happier. Also, I caught the eye of a beautiful girl that most deemed unapproachable because her boyfriend was a star sportsman. She was not only sexy but an upper-class woman at that. Fear of rejection was not a concern this night because I could always say "she wants to know me." My ego would not allow myself to ingest anything else, plus, it was the mental and emotional barrier I needed to proceed if I were to pursue this quest.

Men used this as the last phrase to deal with our insecurities of rejection. After all, it is one thing if we are rejected as a regular guy, but a rock star being rejected was unthinkable. Men always have code sayings that supposedly only men in our inner circle would understand the meaning. Though men never admit that we have insecurities, everyone was quick to adopt this phrase, which in essence means she wants to be my girl but… That *"but"* could be filled with any disclaimer of our ego's choosing. In this instance, my disclaimer if rejected would be to say, "yeah, she wants to know me, but her notable boyfriend (the 'Jock') is blocking me."

This built-in disclaimer provides the courage to approach a girl that one would not normally "swing at." I had previously told some of my friends of my desire to "swing at" this girl and was met with predictable laughter and jokes of "quit dreaming Dunn." After the show, I position myself to come in contact with this typically *standoffish* girl and jackpot, she immediately complimented my performance and gave me that "you're a cute young boy" look. As far as I was concerned, I had reached success because that was enough to fit my "she wants to know me" criteria. Everything that happens from here is icing on the cake. Feeling this victory, I pulled her close to me to show my appreciation and thanks for the compliment-- hugged and kissed her on the cheek.

The next action went beyond my imagination as my tongue was suddenly down her throat and she wasn't resisting at all. As this kiss is happening, I am noticing that I am backstage, and this scene is reminding me of my elementary school kiss. I am expecting her boyfriend to show up and I am not fearful of the ass-kicking I am sure to receive, but I fear she is going to start to kiss him. Reality check, what I am actually fearing is that she is going to cheat on me with her boyfriend. I have just proclaimed this unavailable girl mine. Unbelievable masculine vulnerability. And it's only the first kiss.

My IMAGE!

Image building or protection of image makes for a series of unpredictable emotions and actions. As my popularity or perceived popularity is growing around the "yard" (campus), I am feeling more comfortable with college life. In addition, I am feeling social pressure to have a main girlfriend. Ironically, having a main girlfriend made you more attractive and desirable to other girls who wanted to have that same type of relationship. Of course, they could confide in you and share all their secrets. Though as a freshman I was enjoying being perceived as an upperclassman because of my musicianship, which set me apart and added to the sex appeal. I immediately used this perception to become a great catch for the ladies. The fraternities tried to recruit me, with one offering to forego the pledge process in exchange for my performing at the Greek shows. I turned them down as my performing schedule was too busy.

Most freshmen girls also wanted to have a main college boyfriend, but were too shy and didn't know the parameters of a college life relationship. Most girls had hypothetical high school sweethearts back at home, and to make themselves more attractive to the pursuer they used prom pictures as a crutch to make the male work twice as hard to win their affection. These pics represented that they were spoken for without having to verbalize their actual availability status—it was left to assumption. If they met someone they liked they would simply take the picture down. Now, I labeled these homies irrelevant because the girls were too eager to move forward.

Distant lovers   Dealing with the challenge of distant lovers contained all the insecurities on both sides concerning cheating. I quickly realized that most girls wanted to move on or experiment with having the freedom of college romance or flings. Having no curfews and overnight visits anytime they chose created an atmosphere of total freedom—these girls were away from home for the first time in their life as well and wanted to venture beyond their usual comfort zones. I must admit I took advantage of these opportunities only later to realize they took advantage of me as well. Such as college life goes, I became bored with detaching these girls from their supposed back home boys and began to set my sights on this 'main girlfriend' concept which most upperclassmen were enjoying.

I want to PLAY house.

I wanted to play house with someone. Let me think, who or what kind of girl could I do this with, an upper-class girl? No, she would probably see right through me. Try girls in my inner circle? Naw, too close, remember I want to PLAY house, not become emotionally attached. I convinced myself that the best Decision would be, wait till next year.

Well, the summer would change my plans, and my outlook on life as my stepfather notified me that he wasn't going to pay for my college tuition and that I needed to get a job and maybe attend a community college. Understanding my mother would move heaven and hell to ensure my continuing, his words haunted me as I pledged that I will never need him for anything in life again, in essence, "Fuck him!" My music career couldn't pay for the entire cost, so I took a long walk and cried. I remember standing at a street corner thinking should I jump in front of a car. Again "Fuck him" sentiment won out.

The next day I returned to campus in an attempt to maybe meet with my advisor, Dr. Watson. If he had gone home for the summer, I was going to find him at his house if I had to. Luckily, he was in his office and very surprised to see me. He could see the concern on my face and immediately gave me his undivided attention. I explained to him my situation, and he smiled and said: "Dunn I will take care of this, you are too talented and too valuable to this institution." He looked up my GPA and Dean's list status and immediately gave me a music scholarship which was worth half the tuition.

We then walked to the administration office to apply for a university scholarship to pay the rest of expenses including housing. To top it off, we applied for a student loan for my social life. I thanked Dr. Watson for putting me in that 7:45 AM class, which he thought was amusing but told me that it is a designed strategy to help students attend all classes. That realization made me understand that I must have a plan for life and execute it. It also stuck in my mind that university strategies are controlling me. I decided rather than succumb to the anxiety I felt, I rationalized that they are trying to help me. All my vulnerabilities towards campus life and beyond were gone.

From that day on I looked forward to paying tuition because I actually would collect spending money instead of having the struggling story my classmates had. More importantly, I was now a completely independent man. The look of my stepfather's jealousy will always be memorable as he read the scholarship papers. Through it all, I never told my mother of his words for I feared for her safety.

Sophomore year is here, and I now have college experience on my resume. I have purchased my first car, and my music career is blossoming as I am writing orchestral arrangements on many records.

Unbeknownst to me, I am learning to be a leader because I am accountable for hiring and managing my workers; I hired college musicians to play on all these recordings (giving many an opportunity to expand and meet celebrities). I am the "*paymaster*" and enjoying the fruits of that labor. Uh-oh, I am starting to feel the power of talent. I have tried to remain humble and stable. I knew all too well about how life could change so very quickly. Remember, we were stars in high school and quickly returned to struggling musician status.

Though I was young, I had several big-time clients—I arranged for Bobby Massey and the O'Jay's record label, the prestigious WayOut Records and Epic's Sweet City Records that afforded numerous opportunities to meet other celebrities and so much more. This was huge for a young man under 20.

However, this power seemed to be more stable because I seemed to be in control of my destiny. As a skilled musician, my talent was in demand, and I was putting a lot of people to work. My management skills were sharpening, and I was feeling the transition from boy to man. So, my next plans were to move off campus to an apartment to flex my muscles and start that Playhouse.

During the summer, I had fallen for a young lady name Diane. I pursued her to the point of embarrassing behavior. I openly told anyone that would listen that she was mine. Why, because I said so. She resisted but finally accepted my advances. I didn't mind that she was attending college hours away from me. Secretly I was a little conflicted. Little did she know, that because of my treatment of girls at my school that had distant lovers, made me so fearful of losing her that I rarely went to her campus to visit.

I remember purposely picking a fight with her to break up before she dumped me. As a man, I knew that my girl could easily do to me what those other girls were doing to their theoretical boyfriends back home, and I wasn't willing to sit idly and let that happen to me. I thought the best practice was to be proactive and get ahead of the collision that was bound to happen. I didn't want to discover that Diane was sleeping around – yes, it was a double-standard. However, emotionally, I didn't want to have to face it if, and when, this ugliness reared its head in our relationship. I was simply scared. And now understood that like millions we expend too much energy on things that haven't happened, and sometimes create the avalanche that we were trying to prevent.

In my bravado, no one could reject me...

To her credit, she saw right through that and wouldn't allow me to break up with her. Why, because she said so. Diane became my backbone or crutch with regards to rejection. In my rant, no one could reject me—I wasn't available. Diane was exhibiting some of that unconditional trust, and I respected that. I cared so much for Diane that I put on hold my desire for playing house with a campus girl even though I moved to an off-campus apartment. You see Diane had earned the ultimate status from a man that's referred to amongst his male friends as "my people," which means she is more than a girlfriend, but a friend girl for life. Diane was and remains as "my people."

Maybe two weeks before summer break I had a couple of dates with a perspective prospect for my playhouse campus sweetheart. She had some of the qualities fitting a man with my image. Cheerleader, cute, smart, and great potential arm piece. We laughed and enjoyed each other's company. We naturally hit it off. In hindsight, we both let our guard down because we knew summer was approaching soon and we would go our separate ways.

Well, it seems life takes unexpected turns, and this summer was no different as two things happened that would again change my course. I fell in love, and I joined the mighty, mighty O'Jays! All my masculine vulnerabilities were again front and center.

I had known Karen as a friend from high school and had the opportunity to observe her in other relationships. I liked the fact that she was loyal to her mates even though she would date others. So, I decided over the summer, I would test some unconditional trust traits on her just in case she would become my top prospect. Imagine the arrogance that men exhibit sometime. That's right; I said I would test her like a new car.

Subsequently, throughout the summer while I was definitely loyal to Diane, I portrayed myself to Karen as the perfect understanding, no pressure and absolutely no drama man. No matter what Karen said, or did I offer nothing but support. I spoiled her to a fault. In other words, no other man could compete with this type of unconditional trust because our egos can't handle it. And I mastered the art of displaying what I thought would keep her near and dear to me.

I didn't care to share Karen!

Men are not programmed to allow our woman to be in total control. However, Karen was equally as popular on campus, so this would be difficult if not impossible. I escorted Karen to her

Black Homecoming Queen crowning and I remember thinking "how in the hell am I going to compete with all these guys lurking, shit I'm already dealing with the sportsmen swinging at my cheerleader!" So, in my mind I uttered the words I could handle sharing, but my heart was totally the opposite. Deep down I didn't care to share Karen with anyone, but I had opened the door and did not know how to close it without losing her since she was accustomed to her freedom, and I had mine.

The worst-case scenario would be if Karen slept with another man . . . .

Though I didn't realize it at the time, what I was actually planning to give Karen was what Jackie and partially Diane, had given to me. "Freedom of choice." My goal was to get her to use me as her crutch—to be her "good thing," a term that I later learned from her friends was her term of endearment for me.

I would have the perfect sweetheart, a cheerleader that all men desired and were filled with envy. Both popularities would rise to the ultimate couple status. Yes, some men may be able to swing at Karen but would have to admit that she belonged to Donnie (Dunn).

The worst-case scenario would be that some may even hit a home run but still could never capture her heart. I believed that I could sustain that blow because of course I was *celebrity* and a star myself. Girls would jump at the opportunity to take Karen's good thing as well. And many tried…. It all made perfectly good sense to me.

It's funny how men will seek out attractive women then subconsciously entertain no one else will approach them – women, also do the same thing.

I know Karen knew I was different – she took every advantage of her station in life to develop a prowess for attracting more of what she desired understanding no matter what happened, she could count on me. I was the emotional security blanket with which she could always drape herself from any storm. We occasionally shared fantasies and what the ideal scenario would be for both with the understanding that we were to be open, fair, and return to each other as before.

However, this unconditional support came at a COST. Many of my closest friends especially the guys taunted me with "Man, you need to check your girl" or the macho no words but look of I would never let my girl do this and that. Those sentiments hurt my heart deeply because I knew they were sincere in protecting me. The thought of people gossiping behind my back was overwhelming. What I was too vulnerable to reply was the real answer, "I simply love her". Karen earned every stripe in the badge of my honor because no matter what Donnie did and that was a lot, Karen stood by me with unconditional support and if anybody and I mean anybody would try to hurt or steal Donnie away, Karen by any means necessary was going to protect and keep "her Donnie". At the end of the day, we were simply boyfriend and girlfriend.

Sometimes, what we want just doesn't happen. But as life continues to unfold, we are wise to garner the lessons taught that prepares one for the next dimension, and when we fight change, we are only hindering what is to be.

Road Days –
Sex, Drugs and Rock-n-roll

Dunn & Brucestreet Release Party with the O'Jays

CHAPTER 7

The Road Days

SEX, DRUGS and ROCK-N-ROLL

If I tried to create the perfect

scenario, certainly having a

"Groupie" to lean on

never came to mind . . .

I'm standing backstage at Madison Square Garden awaiting the arrival of my fellow group members and opening act personnel. On my arm is a BEAUTIFUL woman. The kind of "model" beauty that would make any man stop and take notice. This woman was true to that phrase as each member stopped, making a comment or gesture of approval.

Most of the guys spoke by simply calling aloud my nicknames; "Donnie!", "DP!" "Pearson!" "Humpback," "P" ... Phrases such as "Party Tonight"; "Strike"; "Love Train"; "Got to give her what she Wants"; "Backstabbers," and "Let me make Love" were uttered. The ultimate compliment came from our lead singer Eddie Levert, who got down on his knees and bowed to the King while kissing her hand I might add. Mr. Smooth, Walter Williams spoke no words, just smiled of approval. My bosses and musical idols were proud of me!

Even the Isley Brothers (opening act), which entered with a huge entourage wearing furs and minks stopped to nod and slap my hand. The promoter (Dick Griffey/SOLAR RECORDS) came in accompanied by another opening act singer (Carrie Lucas), approached and said: "Ah, that's nice young boy!" I smiled at each one, as very few words were needed as the display spoke for itself. The woman's words were limited to "Hi, nice to meet you" and "Thank you" . . . When they all passed by, this BEAUTIFUL SEXY woman turned to me and commented: "Y'all certainly have your own language."

Okay, before I tell you how my ego was over-inflated, let me reveal what actually had just taken place. Two days prior after a show in North Carolina we were traveling through Virginia and stopped at a truck stop. In those days, we traveled by customized buses that would draw attention. I always looked forward to stopping because it broke up the continuous talk of "who struck who" (I will interpret later), and how great the supposed sexual encounters went. In the mind of every man he was, of course, the greatest lover and the girls could never get enough.

While going to the store, I noticed a *BEAUTIFUL* woman sitting in the back of a car by herself. Understanding that after playing a show, we entertainers experience the feeling, power, and confidence beyond reality that we can do or conquer anything.

She knows how to be a great date.

So, I had no problem approaching her and being direct with my "lines" (conversation). "Hey beautiful, I don't mean no disrespect to Virginia or wherever we are, but you don't look like you belong here" sincerely. I continue, "Why don't you ride with me on our bus and I'll take you to New York." With a smile, she says "Yes, you're right." I pause to hear exactly which line I am right about. She explains that she doesn't live in Virginia, but visiting family. "I actually live in New York and will be flying home tomorrow." JACKPOT!!! I scream, "We are playing 'The Garden' tomorrow, and you must be my guest." We exchange phone numbers.

I left early for the show to meet her at the backstage door. Before the event, I told her "I'll give instructions on how to act when the rest of the group arrives and what to expect"; she smiles and jokes that she knows how to be a great date. As each member passes with comments, what they were really saying was okay Pearson game on tonight!

They challenged me to bring her to the party. The song titles referenced the group's future plans. Dick Griffey was actually saying that because the singer (Carrie Lucas), and I would talk nightly (as friends only). I should never dare to think that I could ever be more to her because I was just a young boy and he was a powerful, rich man. Our lead singer was physically bowing down in anticipation that Pearson had brought a great gift to him. His motto was "Baby, why would you settle for the helping hand when you can have the main man?" The other group was merely wishing me good luck with her surviving this madness.

The most important references dealt with "Strike." This term represented the fact that this

BEAUTIFUL woman is not Karen (my people), so I was open to being "struck." You see we played a game when it came to scoring with girls on the road. The unwritten rules were that unless the girl were your wife or "your people" (significant other), no respect of not hitting (striking) on them would be given. So, each night we would host a "party" which was a rotation of each member's hotel room where all the groupies (women) would gather.

The guys would stop by, pick and choose their date for the evening (no strings attached). If a guy was interested or brought a specific girl to the party and she wound up with someone else, Oh well... This game would have lasting effects as egos, pride and bragging rights made this a high stakes game filled with uncertain emotions. Guys would do unbelievable things to strike someone else. Money, gifts, airplane tickets, sex, drugs, and rock-n-roll—you get the point. L.O.L. Me, being the "*Young*" boy was, in essence, challenging the supposed men to strike if you can.

Soon it was Showtime, and make no mistake in doubting our professionalism; we were always serious about the music. Our entire O'Jays organization was committed to performing at the highest levels. This show of camaraderie produced a male bond that would strengthen with every scream from the 20,000 fans in the audience. After about a month on tour, the show would be so tight that each member knew exactly what everyone else was doing and could anticipate the next notes of the performance. If anyone made a mistake everyone knew and would tease you later as long as the mistake was not detrimental to the overall concert. In that case, a severe chiding would be expected as the replay of the show would be featured on the bus ride.

This show was scheduled strategically to maximize the show tightness. My *newly found* BEAUTIFUL woman had a backstage seat so that I could observe her throughout the show. She was clearly enjoying herself, and I was gaining confidence with every applause and being the envy of the guys. Of course, in between songs, the guys were giving me the "look" while glaring to the backstage onlookers. I believe this bond helped us endure the offstage competition and what I considered "backstabbing." All in all, our friendships would somehow withstand anything or anybody.

On this night, the unspoken game was essentially anti-climactic because after all, this was New York and most guys had plans. So, the strike attempts were quick and delivered with using a football term "Hail Mary." The BEAUTIFUL woman went to my room and delivered a memorable evening that did not include sex. What she did was give me a lesson in the complexity of a so-called groupie. For me, this was my most interesting and challenging experience of being an entertainer.

I could understand a girl being intrigued by me. I thought I was attractive enough to be desired, but I could not understand why the girl would want to have sex with me when she barely knew my name. Again, the promoter was right about one thing, I was the youngest in the band so how to deal with the groupies was something I longed to master, and needed guidance.

I was vulnerable to the wide range of advice versus the actual acts of these passing encounters. The only thing I came to expect was the unexpected. I admit each experience was exciting. This BEAUTIFUL woman sat on my bed and instructed me to sit beside her, which I was eager to do. "I guess you want to kiss me now," she said in a very sexy tone. I nodded yes, and she smiled, and said, "let me put on my kissing lipstick."

During this change of lipstick, she puckered her lips like I have never witnessed in such a sexy way that made me so excited; I thought I would have an orgasm right then. She kissed me, and at that moment I didn't care if she never knew my real name was Dunn or anything else. She gently pulled back, "I know for you the date was over when all your friends conceded that you are King" she mumbled. Oh shit, I thought, she's got the whole thing figured out. I am now nervous about what's going to happen next. She lies on the bed and speaks sincerely, "I loved the way you approached me; direct, yet, kind. I decided to be your groupie tonight."

Relieved, I kissed her again, which I thought was leading to sex or, so I thought. This BEAUTIFUL woman then breaks it down for me which I'll describe as New York style. "I'm ON the bed, but for you to get me IN the bed, you'll have to put up or get up." I'm now insulted.

"You mean I got to pay you? I don't need to buy no sex. Did you see the 20,000 people tonight?" She begins to laugh and says, "I'm here partially because my entire family was so impressed with you, they are all waiting to hear about tonight; c'mon playa, I mean your heart."

Well, my heart stops, and I realize that unlike most groupies this self-proclaimed groupie wanted to communicate with me. She wanted to be treated like "my people" at home where I had to go on dates, meet her parents and really put my vulnerable heart on the line. I was willing to put my pride and ego on the line, but my heart was off limits around this cast of characters.

Karen was "my people," and I had too much invested in my relationship to jeopardize it. I was forced to admit that I was playing and not ready to be serious. What I didn't admit was that over this night I had fallen for this woman, but was too scared to try a long-distance affair with an outgoing New Yorker. The next time I saw this BEAUTIFUL woman was in a fashion magazine.

That encounter changed my future approaches. First, I ceased entertaining negative concepts about groupies; groupie was no longer a negative stereotype. Although up until this encounter, the only references etched in my mind was of women who were willing to have sex just to have access and didn't care if nothing else came with it. Not even a phone call.

But this subtle beauty opened my eyes to see there was a heart on the other side of the encounter that longed to be appreciated. These women were music lovers who wanted to enjoy and experience the lifestyle of musical genius. Second, I had to admit the arrogance in my past treatment of these groupies as objects, though, some seemed to relish being treated that way. From that point, I tried to treat each encounter with a "groupie" with respect seeing the woman as a human being, first. Before we get too googly-eyed, let's not get carried away with any blurred lines, at the end of the night it was just consensual sex. I go my way; they went theirs.

Funny explanation by a groupie . . .

Irrefutably, working in this arena, you can have unbridled access, but that is not necessarily a healthy thing; physically, mentally, or financially. You never want to be the "Jock" with an STD, unwanted pregnancy or having a woman steal your money that wasn't stashed away. Any and all was possible, and there is no way to fake this; you had to be street smart because no matter how charming the women were there was always an opening for any of the above.

My skills of PROBING were always deployed… many women puzzled the hell out of me, so I would always ask the girl, why are you here and why do you want to have sex with me? This directness (New York Style), would rapidly break the barriers of awkwardness. I found that most girls used me (wow, I thought I was using them in our game) to satisfy their fantasy of being with a star. The encounter provided them a chance to be a celebrity to their girlfriends every time our music played on the radio. A funny explanation by a groupie was "My man is always cheating on me, well every time he hears the commercial that Y'all are coming to town, he straightens up."

Most importantly, I broke down my wall of insecurity and vulnerability to the unspoken question, "Does the groupie want the entertainer or the man?" This question had prohibited my enjoying the moments of interactions as my mind and body was never totally relaxed. I realized it was OK if the groupie wanted neither or a combination.

Okay, I thought I had a handle on my encounters until the groupie experience threw me a curve. We would visit most cities twice a year, so these repeat encounters began to develop into more meaningful relationships. This exchange forced my heart to be invested in the ongoing game because of the time, emotion, and financial investment. Now to be "struck," really stung by a groupie was yet to come.

One such groupie shattered my rosy picture I painted of my musical life encounters. Every time I would go to Philadelphia, which was often, Maxine (last name withheld), would worship the ground I walked on. She displayed loyalty in the face of the "strikers" telling her otherwise. She would grab and beg me to fuck her no matter who was present, literally. Mind you, after some time had passed, I thought this woman wanted the man; it'll become clearer. All this finally gained my confidence and trust. Maxine was my Philly girl.

Well a few years after leaving the O'Jays my new group Dunn & Bruce Street has a new record released. Suddenly, I am receiving multiple calls from Maxine to please come to Philly. I finally go, and upon arrival at her house, she greets me with a different atmosphere. Her apartment is candlelit

and smells of tasty food on the stove saturated the room; never had it like this before. Maxine has run a bath for me and invited me to just lie in bed for serving. She has the radio on and to my delight, our song plays three times in an hour representing high rotation.

Okay, now I know why the multiple desperate calls, but this is my Maxine so, I'm cool. Soon dinner is served, and Maxine continues to attend to every possible need I could ever have. I am in shock at the 'heightened' sexual experience she exhibits. I'm beginning not to enjoy what should have been ecstasy on steroids because this groupie is performing like a professional.

Our song title "If You Come With Me" is taking on a different meaning. More important, after all these years of her screaming like I'm King of the pussy, was fake.

I deserve!!

Not being able to control my mouth I ask "Hey, where's all this treatment been before?" I stop myself from uttering, "Oh, because my record is on the damn radio" ... Sensing my frustration, she stops and emphatically states, "You didn't deserve this before. Donnie, I have been with you, displayed undying loyalty, put up with your bullshit and stood behind your precious Karen. I deserve to be your wife, MARRY ME." I arise and walk out the door. I was deeply hurt by a groupie.

I allowed myself to commit to her knowing in the back of my mind that she was a groupie... was my reason for feeling jaded justified? Or am I faced with the reality that women just like men are capable of reserving total access until the right moment?

THE FIRST MAJOR CRISIS

As one can imagine being on the road as an entertainer is filled with so many opportunities for things to go gravely wrong; with so much socializing, books, sex, and booze, it can be a disaster just waiting to happen. Our group, The O'Jays, was no different. We had one of the greatest scares while touring that called for everyone to stop what we were doing and get to the nearest hospital right-a-way.

Our percussionist player had contracted Hepatitis C – a highly infectious communicable disease. Now mind you, prior to learning this, I had just met another young lady in the city where we were performing. Nothing had transpired between us, but as you can visualize, I was leery of getting any closer to this young lady after being told later by the doctor what was the cause of my band member's illness. However, what was shocking to me was, neither of us pressed forward to try to introduce sex into the situation. I actually enjoyed just talking to the young lady.

Well, she and I were talking about numerous of things when I get the phone call that our percussionist fell ill. I made my way to his room and immediately I decided to get him to the nearest doctor as soon as possible. He protested, citing he would probably feel better and just needed to rest. I, however, wasn't hearing any of that. So, I finally prevailed and got him to get medical attention.

Shockingly, the E.R. doctor said to me, "We ran tests, and he has Hepatitis C; call everyone in your band and tell them to get here ASAP. They need to get treated." To me, the scare was real. However, the other guys relegated to their regular; "Pearson, man, I am not going to the doctor. I'll be fine." However, I wouldn't relent and was able to get everyone there except for one principal person; he said he would visit his own private physician after the tour.

What this scare revealed was men are prone to hide behind the shield of invincibility—many men, including myself, who is a stroke survivor, have made a million excuses not to make time for routine checkups. We all think there will be another day—our priorities are often skewed by nonsense.

One of my "stupid excuses" was "I can't afford to be sick" as if I could tell my body a convenient time that would be alright to be ill. Quite frankly, our not going to the doctor is based on FEAR at the core. We are terrified of the *prognosis* because most of us know we haven't been doing the right thing when it comes to our health care. Too often, we do minimal prevention while expecting maximum good health. Though we may beg to differ, Superman, we are not...

I was thinking to myself, I had this attractive young lady, whom I did not know her name, and she really didn't know mine, had the presence of mind to go with me to the hospital. She simply shifted from the role of a "groupie" if you will, to seamlessly step into the role of "caring girlfriend" — to be relevant at the moment. This created another degree of closeness at that time, even though we never had sex we became close. There was a connection. Had I not allowed her to accompany me to the hospital, I would have missed this developmental moment.

Emotionally, I was challenged by her presence just to be there. My EGO normally would have told me to ditch this kind of girl. My inner-self was saying "Man, why are you bringing a damn groupie with you to the hospital. An unknown woman, who probably has slept with so many other men, strange men at that, and you bring her with you. For what?

I learned something about PEOPLE... (GROUPIES). The young lady was just as capable of being genuinely true to care enough just to be there (like a friend would). We were strangers whose paths crossed for a very brief moment. Most people desire to be close to fame, and party with high profile people; it is akin to moths drawn to bright lights, it is mesmerizing, and everybody wants to be up close and personal. She, too, was true to that desire shared by thousands. However, what I was forced to accept was, she, like any other person, was just that, a HUMAN BEING. And I needed to see that. To remove my prejudice and just accept that we are all FLAWED! Including me. I never saw her again.

Most men would effortlessly denigrate the significance of meeting a woman who puts herself out there to connect with a stranger. I wasn't any different. It took years for me to get the lesson; to see a value and extract the positive in lieu of speaking negatively about the young lady . . . It was evident by the outcome that we both just needed real companionship for that moment. Nothing more was needed to suffice.

Truly Masculine Vulnerabilities.

Our Trophy

... it is not what you think !!

CHAPTER 8
PRIZED-POSSESSION

A man's car is his prized-trophy. A car is a sacred possession that represents his public persona, status symbol, self-image, and it's the Achilles Heel of our obsessions. This mirror of perception often leads to irrational decisions and misunderstanding of loved ones, including the people the impression is intended to influence.

The fact is that most men don't understand the significance of this "prized" possession and therefore makes it impossible to accurately explain or show the true sense of connection, and purpose. Women only see a car; men see sex, sex, status, respect, and more pussy. No disrespect ladies, we do think about this. This is why old men, really old guys, drive nice cars that say, "I know you don't want me, but at least enjoy my ride."

Our affixation with the big boy's toy will make us shun family responsibilities and cause a disconnect in the household. We sometimes won't think twice about the investment of time spent on the car; it's akin to a junky who must get his next fix by any means necessary by over washing, waxing and dishing out excessive amounts of cash for accessories that we may or may not need. In our mind, the car needs attention.

We are fascinated with an inanimate object that gives us pleasure and pride; almost organismic, though no man would relate his affinity to a car this way. However, you can assess by our approach and overindulgence that we are getting some degree of satisfaction. No matter how synthetic it is, we will dedicate our time as if to a longtime lover that we don't want to be lonely.

Eventually, we walk away when a fragment of fulfillment is obtained. Seriously, we are enamored – can't see anything, don't want to hear anything, and please don't ask us to do something other than what we are engrossed in at that moment . . . It's personal. And yes, it's a man's thing. It is similar to when men have great sex;

the fix is on, and we don't stop until that need is satisfied.

REALLY? A-FREAKIN' CAR...

This state of hidden confusion is often used as a weapon; it is an explosive source at the core ego of a man. In men talk, a common remark is: "They always say I care more about my car than . . ." What is absent in men talk is the acknowledgment that we may forget birthdays and anniversaries, but we remember all the details of our prized trophies, especially cars.

Now, I am a member of the O'Jays' orchestra, my choice of car is no exception to my analysis of a man's prized-possession; however, there is one problem, I am still in college which could affect my personal choices. Now, to match my perceived entertainer's persona, the choices were: Cadillac, Mercedes, or Rolls Royce. Well, the latter was out the question. However, Walter Williams, one of the lead singers had purchased 2 Rolls Royces and called me to offer taking one of his Mercedes. It was an offer too good to be true, but, before I said yes, absolutely or any other phrase "hell yeah" came out my mouth.

I remember him being in utter shock when "no" was my actual response. You see me being the youngest in the organization and college, I thought I wasn't ready to appreciate such an expensive car . . . For one thing, both of my parents owned Cadillacs, and I treated those cars without proper respect . . . But the biggest reason for saying NO was that I knew being on a college campus if I drove a Mercedes, I would turn into a chauffeur as none of my friends would ever drive again and anywhere we went, I would have to pay. I simply wanted to fit in as a regular student. So, my choice was a Chrysler Córdoba; a popular car due to the advertising campaign headed by the TV "Fantasy Island" show star.

I kept my car cleaned and always in top mechanical shape—it was just the right choice for college life. Unequivocally, it was a big hit with both boys and girls. At one point my two roommates Bernard and Walter "Slu" had new cars as well, so to visit our place was like going to a new car lot *the boys had it going on!*" The unspoken game of one-upmanship between men is based on using the car as an image tool.

The Córdoba featured "Corinthian Leather" which I bought clothing outfits to match the color. To further enhance my image and status, I traded that car in for a brand new one as soon as next year's model was available to show that I was a new car man. Always the latest and greatest for me. Though I loved the status symbol, I sometimes felt my shiny car was outshining me.

Well, one day, another client Glen Covington (accomplished singer and noted nightclub entertainer), arrived at my door unannounced proclaiming "today you are going to buy a Cadillac

". . . I remember thinking he can't be serious, however, realizing he just drove almost 2 hours to get to me I began to take him seriously. I asked why a Cadillac and why today. Well, he explained that he had landed a new production deal for us and I needed to upgrade my image, so off we went to the dealer. He had already secured a salesman and soon after I was the new owner of a Cadillac Seville. I cherished this car in terms of my care for the vehicle and the upgrade in my personal image, but make no mistake it was still just another car as I was so used to driving Cadillacs.

One day I'm about to leave for tour, and my father calls to borrow my car . . . My father was always so proud of his car, but unfortunately no longer had his Cadillac and with his heavy drinking, I was reluctant to say yes. All the times he had given me his car to drive and was probably equally as reluctant because of my age, but how could I say no—I remember thinking let me empty the car as I took my horse gear out of the trunk.

Upon my return, my father gave me a story of how my car was stolen, which later I found out that his best friend had taken my car and sold it!! He was so jealous that my father had a son whom could afford such a possession that he wasn't sorry, but felt the opposite and told my father "your son has insurance; he can buy another one." My father never spoke to him until his friend was on his deathbed or close to it. Was a Cadillac worth a lifelong friendship? Well little did I know, but I was about to discover further the value placed on a car... It's a lot deeper than you can imagine.

I get a replacement Cadillac, didn't really like this one for the Seville was no longer in manufacturing and I got an Eldorado. I am driving through Pennsylvania on my way home from tour and stopped to get gas. A young white boy is pumping the gas and asks, "Hey, you must be a sports player." I respond no . . . He continues, "Oh, you must be an entertainer." Again, I respond no. Becoming frustrated with my answers or shall I say non-answers, he begins popping his finger as if to suggest he is trying to remember where he has seen me and said, "I know. I have seen you on television."

The gas attendant's incessant questioning made me increasingly irritated because I know he is trying to find out how this young black nigger can afford this car while he has to pump gas, and my reluctance to share my profession didn't inspire him to make the banter any easier . . . I could hear the frustration in his voice of I'm the reason why his life is miserable . . . (in my mind) I again respond no, that's your issue.

Never realized white men felt this way.

Now he is downright mad and unable to mask his seething frustration says "Oh, I know what you do" and rubs his nose implying that I'm a drug dealer. I gave him the fuck you look while pulling out a wad of cash to pay for the gas. Even though I am an entertainer, I would have said yes if he had said aren't you a doctor or school professor. Why must black men be stereotyped? I will never forget his last words to me "nice car."

I drive away, continuing down the highway, about thirty miles my car begins to sputter, and as I pull off to the side of the road, the car shuts off. Being pre-cell phone days, I had to walk about half a mile to use an emergency phone to call the police. Soon the officer arrives, and I begin to tell him about needing a tow service. The officer cut me off and starts to question me 'ala' driving while black stop; "registration, insurance card, any weapons in the car." He begins to circle the car and says, "nice car."

After reviewing my documents, he merely says, "Oh, I'll radio you a tow truck" and leaves. I wait two hours before realizing no help was coming. I walk about two miles to a public pay phone and call my mother, who drives three hours to get me.

I get the car towed and later discover that the gas station attendant mistakenly (yeah right), put leaded gas in my unleaded vehicle burning out the catalytic converter. The car was never drivable again, so I moved into the BMW car family. Total masculine vulnerabilities! This white boy was that jealous of a car to ruin it. The officer was that envious that this young black boy could legally be the owner of such a trophy and left me in danger. Perhaps a prized-trophy he could not afford—but one I earned to drive.

For the record, over the years, I was later stopped more than 30 times superfluously while driving black. And facing so many indignities that finally I began to tell each officer right at the beginning of the supposed "weaving stop," that I don't drink and if you want to search me or the car just, please be man enough to say that at the onset. And just do that without the charade of having me walk a line and put my finger on my nose. To their credit, if I must say so, 95% of the officers appreciated my appeal to their manhood and would still search the car, but wouldn't subject me to the usual bullshit tactics to proceed with a search while denigrating my prized trophy!

I tell you every time they would give me that fake compliment of "nice car" made me willing to die for my car. Thank God, I placed more value on my responsibility to live.

A CHANGE is coming …

CHAPTER 9

Change of Life

(Kent, OH to New York City)

Any person who has experienced a geographical change knows it can be the biggest paradox of life; you are excited but scared. The transition can be hopeful, yet, filled with extreme uncertainty and feels overwhelming simultaneously. Whereas you possess a knowing that somewhere over that rainbow is the world you've dreamt of where one's loftiest dreams do come true, folks will know your name and your star will rise, and then there is that voice that whispers "Are you sure?"

I felt all the above; the move to the BIG APPLE was colossal. Being in the coveted entertainment Mecca in the Northern Hemisphere where you garner respect beyond one's wildest imagination, and dreams do come true for those willing to vie and take their place in the spotlight . . . was nothing less than daunting and fulfilling because I was on my own. Somebody more prominent than before called my name this time and that, which I left, had no influence on the decision. It was empowering.

As a young adult, it wasn't long before I had to settle in my mind there were a lot of things that had to change; the culture and pace in New York were different and commands you *"get"* with it or be left behind. You really have to be a quick study. And that meant I had to be open to help – new ideas, contemporary trends, and people who either were going to help me develop and expand my talent or, try to hurt me by restricting access.

I was scared.

Initially, there were so many things I overlooked because I was so excited to start fresh and secure a new corner of the market in the music industry. While at the same time I was scared and a little saddened to leave what was familiar and routine. And being the only child and a male, how would my mother manage without me. Okay, maybe I'm just a little dramatic, but I am the only child and who else would think these thoughts.

Although she is remarried to a wonderful man, my stepfather, Lloyd, who would never allow anything to disrupt her happiness, though, I still felt an obligation to make her smile in any way humanly possible.

I was well established in Cleveland and Kent, Ohio as a producer, arranger, and composer nevertheless, a new opportunity was presented, and naturally, my instincts would never allow me to shut a door before exploring all the possibilities. After all, if it didn't work out, I could always return home.

In Kent, I had a routine, one that worked for me and now starting over in a new place, with new people posed just as many problems as it would opportunities. However, what was calling and speaking to my soul was stronger than what I was holding onto back in Ohio. And many times, in life we have these divine nudges to get up and out of that which is familiar because what awaits is far more rewarding, but will never know unless you let go. So, I did.

STICKER SHOCK!!

In Kent, I lived near the college campus and had roommates—my share of the rent was only $90 per month. Can you imagine how my heart rhythm accelerated when I had to adjust to paying $650 for an apartment in the Big Apple by myself? I was going through the motions at 25 yrs. old; thoughts of returning to Ohio were amusing.

However, the ship had sailed, and my journey of being a man was tested on every level. I always wanted to make my unique mark in the entertainment world; for so long I played behind the scene, arranged, and produced for renowned artists and sometimes was overlooked and cheated out of my credits as a producer, writer, and arranger. I found myself having to fight twice for what was already earned – imagine that. What a paradox?

On several occasions, opportunities that should have been mine were sabotaged by some prominent artists when record executives inquired about the work on specific tracks. I found out from one record executive in Philadelphia many years later that he had personally inquired about the arranger on several of the songs their label had recorded, and each time he was told that it was someone other than me.

A few artists that I worked with would just lie and give credit to someone else just to keep me from moving on to bigger projects. Their intentional plan to confine my influence infuriated me, and I didn't let that go (there wasn't any way I would gloss over this bullshit) . . . It got ugly!! And I didn't care how it ended.

A few narrow-minded motherfuckers were toying with my destiny, years of commitment and discipline invested, and in essence, were attempting to derail why God gave me the gift (to share with the world) in the first place.

Though, I had to process my nostalgia—As my mother's only child, the bond was felt even stronger; what I came to appreciate very early was the investment my mother, "mom"

grandmother, Alverna Mayfield and piano teacher Mrs. McManning, all women, in my life made.

In this new environment, I would extract from many of the lessons they taught me—persistence, hard work, faith. To believe, believe, believe. Always, believe.

It was a priority to make my mother proud because she was always present in my journey; from touring with the Ponderosa Twins, shows with James Brown, Al Green, Jackson Five, Lola Falana, the Moments and of course, as a college kid, playing for the O'Jays . . . she never missed a beat. She was and is the prototype of what I look for in a woman; a partner.

Being in New York has a vibe that is unmatched; there is no comparison anywhere in the United States – the energy is so massive and captivating that it sucks you in. It's so easy to lose track and bounce around if your goals aren't concrete and you lack a strong work ethic. As a young male entertainer, the entrapment was magnified: Girls, girls, girls, and more beautiful, sophisticated, available girls. It's the fly in the ointment–you may need it, but not all the time and so learning to balance my new position was crucial.

I loved the attention, not primarily just from women, but the industry executives; the business folks recognized that I brought a unique style and quality to the table. It's where every young musician and artist long to be…called upon and requested. The sophisticated modern-day term is "MONETIZED!"

It wasn't long before I had to settle what would be my rhythm in the APPLE – I had folks making plans for me, about me, both professional and personal and I wasn't okay with that. See I was still the forceful buck that called the shots and had the talent and confidence to match my passion. I imagined many folks were nervous about my approach. It was difficult to give others control – what I fought against wasn't necessarily a bad thing, but my ego wasn't mature enough to process everything as smoothly as I should. I was tired of people taking from me, and I refused to be denied. Especially, when I felt I was being held back again because of some twisted, manipulative ideology promoted by those who didn't measure up.

In my mind, it was time to run free, to touch the world and make people happy with my gift, and not succumb to the narrow-mindedness of another group of ideologues censoring me. Specifically, those with less or no skills in my discipline; it drove me crazy. I guess we call this

Déjà vu – there was no way I would settle to exist in a world where abundance flows and not get mine. Instinctively, I knew how to maneuver around limited-thinking people, I was just hoping that it wouldn't have to be deployed so soon.

The other major hurdles being in New York didn't have anything to do with women, it was fighting off men that approached me secretly because they were on the down-low. This territory was uncomfortable and different for me. The art crowd was open and feeling-oriented, displaying various forms of loving. I'm okay with people being who they are. I worked hard to make sure they, just like several women would not be able to stand in my way because my 'NO' to their advances were not well received. I didn't care to be a part of any of their constructed decisions to entrap me (male or female).

This wasn't any different from the way some women who plotted to either date me or try to manipulate our relationship in a way that was just not going to happen. A few times I recall working late in the recording studio and the phone would ring. Butch Jones (Grammy award-winning engineer) would say "it's for you" in a musical tone that didn't exist. I automatically knew it was a particular female calling with a trumped-up hardship so that I would leave work, only to arrive at her residence and nothing was wrong. Such silly games that were so unnecessary and only diminished the attraction I had for her.

Ladies, a man will never *construe* faking distress as light-hearted and flattering; no matter if we have passionate sex after getting down to the truth, it is still nonsense. We see your behavior on a deeper level as a *menacing* aspect of your personality: Conniving and manipulative. And since we don't trust that it will end there and not escalate to something bigger, we bank that data.

Though nothing more may ever be said about it, don't ever think we are not moving farther and farther away from you before the door finally closes behind us with no return in mind. Being physically present doesn't guarantee that he is with you because men always leave first mentally.

Sexual Openness in the Apple . . ..

What is over the top as a man where I felt a different kind of male-on-male vulnerability that I was not opened to or previously experienced is when three renowned male celebrities approached me.

One, a noted author and playwright, then there was the distinguished Broadway choreographer and, a legendary jazz singer. Most men are too macho ever to admit being confronted with male-on-male vulnerability because it's very uncomfortable if you are heterosexual. I'm from Cleveland, and we were not as socially open as the people were in New York City during this time. If a man hit on you sexually, this kind of interaction was typically met with hostility. For me, I was vulnerable because as a composer and producer, I had to work with these men who apparently were attracted to men and I didn't want to offend them.

So, I swallowed my pride about a lot of things they said and did, and just focused on my job; I was in New York to work.

The jazz legend's inquest and probing into whether I was interested was painstaking only because we were performing together on the same show in a stadium and had to walk back across the field together to enter the tunnel, which allotted more time for him to make his propositions. He was working hard. I tried to act like it didn't bother me but was also suppressing thoughts of knocking the hell out of him if he touched my butt or rubbed me the wrong way.

The conflict was I really liked this guy's music, hell, the world did. This man was a phenomenal singer bar none, and I would hate to be on record for beating his ass because he went too far pushing his preferences. Plus, I am not a violent person and prayed that he would just move on and leave me the hell alone. Why he had to blur the lines I'll never know; he was one of my music idols, and I wasn't feeling his insistent behavior to entice me. I was just honored to play on the same world stage backing him up and wanted nothing more.

INDIRECT ENCOUNTER . . .

I had the great honor of recording and signing Tony Award Winner Melba Moore to my label Believe Music Works, distributed by Lightyear/Warner/Elektra/Atlantic. The experience with this icon crossed many plateaus including professional and personal. Melba was in the midst of a nasty divorce with a man that many said we had semblances of both looks, and characteristic.

Balancing my private opinions was challenging to say the least and indeed forced many male vulnerabilities. How do I agree with the male bashing while disagreeing with the premise of many issues? I found that like most women, I had to choose the times to LISTEN and the opportunities to COMMENT!

I admire most that Melba is a survivor with strong tenacity. One night we are driving downtown in the city and she says "Dunn, pullover and let's go in here." I don't know if this was pre-planned, but the next thing I know, Melba has pulled out a mini tape recorder and begins to sing. We must have sold nearly a hundred CDs as most customers bought 5 - 10 copies in support of this talented legend! I will never forget the call to my college homey *Bernard* declaring, "Man you won't believe how many "hit" (approached) on me tonight."

"Hey, Man, how many of the girls do you have with you now?' he asked after hearing my excitement. I responded "None"; cracking up, for we were at the LGBT center and the men loved Melba and desired me. We both laughed hysterically because this had never happened before in such an open fashion.

DOUBLE DOSAGE

The other two encounters happened simultaneously; I'll make this quick. The two gentlemen whom I worked with on a major production, both asked if they could kiss me on the cheek. It was opening night on Broadway and emotions were high, but in a split-second, I had to assess do I insult them by saying something offbeat or just allow these two openly gay celebrities to kiss each cheek on my face.

Recognizing I was very uncomfortable with the request, one of them said, "Dunn, I know you are not gay, we love you, we love your work and just want to give you a kiss." I chuckled, then, looking at both of them as they were standing in front of the door that led to the stage, laughed and said, "Okay, go ahead." They were overjoyed and moved on. That was over-the-top. But it was New York. And we were on BROADWAY!

I didn't see that coming . . .
This was tough!

CHAPTER 10
THE BIG MOMENTS –
Tough Issues

Tough issues reveal the inner power of a man. There is nothing else that will drive us to show up or shut up....

Throughout life men are constantly preparing for the big moments; without warning, life presents tough issues that intertwine and intersect with big moments, complicating the advanced-preparation. There is a wide range of big moments from the first date to marriage, to confronting a threat to self and family, so the preparation is endless. Tough Issues generally will deal with how a man reacts to a given situation such as what to do when your girl doesn't answer the late-night phone call, to whether or not to lie to mom when asked a tough personal question. All influences contribute to how we prepare and actually act in big moments.

You Don't Know Until You Know

The reality is that no matter what the preparation entails our actions are totally unpredictable. So, in the end, these moments are filled with hope and uncertainty or vulnerabilities. I likened it to a trained policeman hoping never to discharge his weapon or a firefighter hoping never to have to fight a fire. Unfortunately, life often requires action and believe me we are totally uncertain of the outcome. These are examples of job-related moments which after experiencing these high anxiety situations a few times, we can handle them with more confidence although the result still may be uncertain.

The challenge is that most big moments don't provide the opportunity to experience this life altering condition until they happen. Being nervous is an emotion we can't pre-prepare for, so we factor that in our thoughts. Ladies, if you are with a man and he start to panic, please don't interrupt the process as we are simply taking a brief second to assess our next action and allowing the nervous moment to pass. In fact, try to remain calm and speak in a reasonable tone; the last thing we need is an erratic partner who is emotionally unstable.

Having that sense of support your man will normally react in the way you hope your protector-in-chief should. A man will choose his mate based on his perception of you in the moments of crisis and triumphs. Nothing drives a man away faster than if he feels you did not (*appropriately*) support him at the moment when he needed you the most. Trust and believe during a crisis is not the time to question our actions. If the action we are taking is not blatantly wrong or harmful, we expect full compliance. There is plenty of time "after the fact" for open discussion. What men talk about to each other is how our women have a whole lot to say when things are "down" but don't say anything when things are "up" and we are playing Santa Claus. What you don't know is many times we have sacrificed a lot to fulfill that false premise of "*everything is great*" because we fear the loss of dignity and abandonment.

Now, these moments I just described often are considered "life and death" or "life or death" situations. The and/or for me has never been clarified in my mind for death is a part of life so, I guess that's why as a child I had a tremendous fear of funerals. I remember when my father's dad passed, and I couldn't make it down the aisle. I cried and screamed so loud my family decided to leave me home for future ceremonies. It wasn't until a class in college where students went behind the scenes or undercover to expose the emotional exploitation of loved ones for financial gain by funeral homes that cured my fear. When my step-brother Benny passed, I couldn't believe how I spoke up, and consequently, the family depended on me to step up in the big moment and handle all the tough issues.

The understanding of a man can be easily defined and connected to big moments in life and tough issues. I am no different.

May 4, 1982 – For my Kent State Alumni, May 4th represents the anniversary of the killing of four protesters of the Viet Nam War. So, I always awake with a salute to their memory. The workday started with my best friend and my music partner of our group Dunn & Bruce Street, planning our promotional tour song lineup (repertoire).

My best friend Bernard (Sax), whom I met in college, had been my roommate and we knew each other's secrets and certainly knew every detail of our relationships. Bruce, I hadn't known a long time as T-Electric Records president, Jim Tyrrell had recently put us together as a writing and producing team. Now we had recorded an album and our single "If You Come With Me" was moving up the charts.

The door opened . . .

We were sitting in my NY, Queens apartment which I took over from Kim about ten months prior. Bruce's girlfriend was a matchmaker or as I teased, "always looking for a way to keep track of Bruce," matched me with her cousin, Kim. This introduction, of course, would lead to deeper things that encompassed numerous bittersweet moments—More sweet than bitter.

Kim was a nice lady... very caring, not clingy, she had her own rhythm and set of friends to occupy her time. And after getting to know her a little better, to my total surprise offered me to stay with her. I didn't know anyone in NY other than the record company family that brought me to the Big Apple, the extended working colleagues and my music partner Bruce.

As a young, thriving musician, it was never my intention to be involved in any manner that would impede my progress. However, Kim represented an openness as a bridge builder; I was still traveling back and forth to Ohio because of contractual obligations with music clients so, her generosity provided me familiarity—a sense of routine when I came back to NY instead of always having to book a hotel.

I was slowly getting used to NY hospitality to share space . . . Often because of the high cost of living New Yorkers were more open to accommodate shelter. I am from Cleveland, the culture there is different, so I was taken aback by such kindness, and trying to maintain my coolness was difficult. I didn't realize until her offer that Mr. Playboy had never actually lived with a woman other than my mother.

It was overwhelming, intertwined with mixed feelings. All my plans of playing house were now front and center as I struggled to reply. My instincts said no, however, my curiosity and desire to "fit in" the New York lifestyle said yes.

Bruce, my music partner, never had his own apartment as he would move from **_friend-to-friend_**, even being the catalyst for my losing one of my upper-end apartments for violating the occupancy rules. To ease my apparent reluctance to move in with someone I had only known a short time, Kim explained that her job was moving her to Chicago soon and this would also provide the closeness to the "Matchmaker" (her cousin), and Bruce who lived in the building as well.

She was right, the four of us played cards, drank nightly and always had a good time bonding.

Kim was extremely accommodating to my needs in transitioning and respected my privacy. I, in turn, was very supportive of her career and personal needs.

We became comfortable with each other, but since I was still commuting back to Cleveland for projects, I would always pack all my belongings and take with me each time. One day the matchmaker told me Kim thought that was crazy. I realized that I was simply attempting to maintain my independence and of course, being non-committal to the relationship that we both knew would end soon. I always thought that our relationship was transient . . . There was no need to tether either of us to unsustainable commitments.

As planned, the day came for Kim to move to Chicago. She was sharing the moving truck with a couple of co-workers that were also being transferred. As her last box was loaded, I remember the awkward moment of saying goodbye because we never discussed any future plans for communicating, let alone where she was going to live. A hug and kiss would suffice. I received only one call "of made it safe," and that was it. I didn't know whether I should feel some kind of way because my ego just assumed I would hear from her daily. Oh well, she didn't, and I didn't. Welcome to New York, I thought—Continue the journey, Dunn....

Back to May 4th. I was excited to review the chosen songs for our show, so we decided to go to the record store to purchase the cover songs (recorded by other artists). Upon returning to the apartment while reading the album credits, my heart suddenly stops, and I am speechless as I read a dedication to my "Karen" from one of my musical idols, Stevie Wonder.

Unconsciously, I disregarded the fact that I am sitting in the apartment that I had lived with Kim, and I still dare to consider Karen "my girl."

Coupled with the fact that Karen has been living in California for years, I am devastated. The news of her having a relationship with this entertainer was not a surprise at all; it was the fact that now everyone in my perceived world knows including my two friends sitting in front of me wondering what the heck is going on.

When I read aloud the credit, Bernard knew precisely what it meant to me, and he just shook his head. However, Bruce didn't know the degree of my past relationship with Karen, so he made a very distasteful comment that men do in these situations, which I didn't appreciate but mustered a fake laugh to save face.

My mind is no longer on our show music. Instead, I'm now consumed with how I am going to respond to the expected avalanche of calls and comments I am about to encounter. My life is now facing a BIG MOMENT!

I try to pretend it did not bother me, so Bruce gets me back to the show music while Bernard is staring at me. With no modern technology, such as caller ID, text messaging and cell phones, every time the phone rings I jump with nervousness expecting to have to confront the Karen crisis as I have labeled it in my mind. Sure enough, the phone rings and I don't recognize the caller's voice.

My heart is racing because I am thinking maybe this is someone who is going to test my emotions about Karen, which I was not anywhere prepared to deal with. To my surprise, the caller was one of Kim's co-workers that had moved to Chicago with her. I hadn't spoken to him since the day they moved so now I am bracing myself for the purpose of the call.

"Hey, Dunn. I am calling to let you know" . . . My blood pressure must have been incalculable as I hear these words, "Dunn we think Kim is in the hospital having a baby" ... My response in hindsight was *facetious* and terse to be exact. "What do you mean you think?" He explained that Kim was not showing (not a big pregnant stomach), but the little bulge she had was characterized by Kim as a female problem that may have to be handled by her doctor.

He further explained that no one had seen or heard from her all day and everyone at the office had called around to hospitals to locate her whereabouts. Certainly, as a newly transferred employee to Chicago gone missing, her employer and co-workers must have been hoping for the best but preparing for the worst. I explained to him that I hadn't heard from her since the day they moved and he emphatically sighed "Ah, uh," as if he now understood why like putting a puzzle together.

He told me he wasn't surprised I hadn't heard from her, but based on the confirmation of her admission at a hospital, they had finally located her and the ward she was in; he felt compelled to call me. Short backstory— there were some sticky issues that I don't care to mention here, but I took control upon my arrival at the hospital to rescind arrangements that were done without my knowledge. At any rate, this call probably lasted about 1 minute. However, it felt like a lifetime.

I am now in the truly BIG MOMENT of my life. Bernard is eagerly anticipating the news of the call as he was observing my emotions while Bruce remained inattentive. I announce the nature of the call, and as I am talking, I realize that I am in shock, but now in *man-up* mode or on *autopilot*. I am no longer thinking, but reacting to the situation using all the tools I had been taught to deal with life lessons in the big moments.

My instincts developed during childhood automatically kicked in, and I began to focus clearer with every passing second. I picked up the phone to call the airlines and then quickly hung the phone up as it didn't matter what time the next flight departed, I was heading to the airport.

Never would I imagine being presented news like this, but was determined enough to fly to where

the young lady was to learn what role I play in this
if any.

Going on blind faith ...

I grabbed a few items as Bruce went to tell
Kim's cousin (who lived upstairs) the news, she
immediately came to my apartment. She had a smile
on her face which I didn't know whether that meant
she knew Kim was pregnant, or just happy I was
going to Chicago. At any rate, I didn't have time to
care.

I reached the airport and was able to secure a
flight that was leaving in 30 minutes. I am filled
with anxiety as the plane takes off and engrossed in
thought I blocked out any safety directions given by
the flight attendant, or who any of the passengers
were surrounding me. I have so many questions,
WHY didn't she tell me she was pregnant? Could it
be that I am not the father? If that's the case, what
the fuck am I doing on this plane in the first place?

Checking myself first, I know I had conducted myself as a perfect gentleman, never so much as raising my voice in any negative tone; we didn't have that kind of relationship. We never argued. Is my baby a boy or girl? Is it mine? What the fuck is happening–I went in blind faith, believing somehow, I was connected to this little bundle of love sent from above.

What should I say to her? All of sudden the thought that changed my course came to me, Dunn, nothing matters except the baby! Now my emotions are settling, the angst I initially harbored was subsiding that enabled me to handle the task at hand. In this short spanned of time, I evolved emotionally. I grew up; manned up and became an adult on this flight.

This 2-hour journey proved to be the most critical time in my life. As I rode to the hospital, I smiled upon realizing that I had absolutely no feelings towards the Karen crisis. What I thought was so important entirely became a non-issue in a matter of minutes. It would be a lifelong lesson for me.

Walking into the hospital, I am nervous and not sure what to expect, but am confident I need to be here. My first stop was the nursery to see what the nurse told me was a girl, which I immediately corrected her with "you mean my daughter." Wow! I am feeling like a devoted father. All the same, the elephant in the room is I also feel so damn conflicted knowing that I am about to go into Kim's room. My angst returned: What if she tells me that I am not the father as the reason why she never informed me of the pregnancy in the first place. How in the hell am I going to handle that if this is the outcome? ... am I too presumptuous?

I pledge to this Gift from God that I
will be the best father . . .

Lessons learned at church while playing the piano, i.e., the priest would espouse on many Sundays how to be a good father, and the need to live a productive life occupied every moment as I recalled my early exposure to these tenets. Here is my perfect storm and though my love of music kept me entrenched in church attendance, God knew those moral lessons I heard would one day come back when the recall was most needed.

Those insignificant moments from years past suddenly were pivotal.

The baby was so precious in my eyes; upon seeing her, I instantly understood why God gave me the talent to play the piano. The big picture wasn't to play an instrument, but the lessons I would learn while playing in church every Sunday. All the teachings that are now in the front of my mind. I pledged to this Gift (my baby) from God, that I will be the best father I could be. I knew I didn't have all the tools, but I vowed to try. As my daughter cried, my eyes well up and I turned around and like a movie script the doctor appeared.

Glad to See *You* . . .

He introduced himself and proclaimed his happiness to see me. He told me that he encouraged Kim to contact me and assured me that she was just scared. Apparently, she was conflicted too about calling me. Of course, I cannot deny thinking if she planned to keep this a secret. If so, why and for how long?

As an entertainer, I want readers to understand; we are confronted a lot with women trying to position themselves to have a baby... those are the ones who immediately broadcast to the world that they are carrying your baby, even if it's not your child. However, I've lived long enough to trust my gut... my gut told me that I should be here.

The look in the doctor's eyes gave me the affirmation that I was doing the right thing. It reminded me of my college advisor and his staunch support during a turbulent period in life, and I gained strength to carry-on. As I reached to shake the doctor's hand, he instead gave me a hug that began to shatter my sturdy, manly exterior. I wanted to cry. I thanked him again and again as he walked away.

Afterward, I walk towards Kim's room, and without hesitation, I enter. She is lying in bed looking extremely vulnerable, weak and worn. I realized at that moment that this lady had opened her door to me as well as her heart. As a vulnerable man, this was so reassuring.

I am not sure whether she is surprised to see me, but I sensed she is waiting for my reaction and first words. I wanted to assure her that everything was and will be okay. I was determined to speak from my heart. She seemed to be relieved as I stated that it didn't matter why she never called, the tension began to subside between us. I pride myself that I have *NEVER* asked her WHY? Ever. The only thing that mattered was how we prepare to be parents from this point forward.

After the small talk of how are you, I addressed several tough issues: Immediate baby care needs, support personnel etc., many issues were awkward because we had never discussed establishing a life together. Unequivocally, I was conflicted. We were both in transition; she moved to Chicago, and I was still working in New York and had several contractual obligations in Ohio and traveled extensively producing other groups. A formula that would make the new addition to our lives a little complicated being away from home most of the time. I guess the best way to say this is "initially we had no plans to continue."

The last thing I wanted to do was drill this woman. However, it was excruciating to overlook the elephant in the room that I did not want to sweep under the rug. Anybody who knows me, know that I like to address shit. Put it on the table and then make a decision. I like FREEDOM to choose. But that is impossible when you don't have all the facts.

I felt defenseless not knowing what were the missing pieces, but I at least wanted to be open to learning why without rushing to judge. I was vulnerable too. But what if this young lady was just trying to spare me pain and I just showed up unannounced?

I am trying my damn best to be present—if, this baby is mine, there was no way I can leave this woman by herself or my daughter for that matter. But I do need to catch my breath.

So, I said, "Kim, you have had nine months to have thoughts of preparation at least, I am going to need a little time to get adjusted." She just gazed at me.

Without strength to ask . . .

"What is this about; we have always talked, why couldn't you tell me?" Echoed in my heart, but I was without strength to say this to her. I only wanted to satisfy the longing to know **WHY!** Why was this a secret? And course, I had to examine myself too.

I could see this woman was scared, just as I was... the last thing I wanted her to worry about was having support. Before leaving, I wrote a check to cover the immediate expenses in addition to flying in a family member to assist her.

As some other issues were addressed, we became more comfortable in talking. We chose the name Denee Michelle Pearson, and soon I was hugging her to leave. As the strain was lessening, it was clear that I flew in hastily and forgot to make hotel accommodations. I was so focused on seeing this little new baby—simply forgot. I didn't know where to go, and just like the beginning of our relationship, Kim offered her apartment and car to me. I laughed as I had no idea where she lived. When she left New York, we only spoke once; she never wrote . . . I never called. It was as if what we shared didn't happen (I guess we were both just living in the present).

So, eventually, I make my way to her new apartment in Chicago and get settled in to collect myself before leaving to go back to work…this was a big moment and I didn't have all the answers.

Heaven kissed the earth.

As I sat on her couch, I am reflecting on this most memorable day: May 4, 1982. I had experienced every manly emotion (as LIFE can change in a flash). What seems to be important and earth-shattering may not be anything at all except our self-absorbed male ego. All in all, I am proud and relieved. I catch my breath and finally begin to exhale.

What a day filled with the ULTIMATE MASCULINE VULNERABILITIES!

The gift from GOD!

My daughter, Denee Michelle Pearson.

ABOUT THE AUTHOR

In today's competitive music field, it's rare for an artist to do it all: Compose, arrange and produce a musical piece. Dunn, is an Award-winning Composer and Arranger, lauded as one of the top African American music composers to have major success in all genres of entertainment along with such notables as Quincy Jones and Bernard Drayton to name a few in Movies, Television, Broadway, Music, and Commercials.

Professionally known as the "Black Beethoven," his scoring credits include: the docudrama "Unhinged" (based on his own journey), the theme of the Fox TV smash "New York Undercover," the HBO movie "Head Office," Columbia Pictures box office hit "The Professional," Miramax's "Ride", Mario & Melvin Van Peebles "Identity Crisis," the faith-based "Iniquity" and the Cinecom Int. Film, starring Oscar winner Geraldine Page, and featuring Oprah Winfrey, "Native Son." He orchestrated and arranged the Broadway Musical, "Amen Corner."

In the studio, this accomplished pianist has produced, arranged, written, and worked with such recording artists, as The O'Jays, Stephanie Mills, Teddy Pendergrass, Stevie Wonder, Mtume, Roy Ayers, D'Angelo, Mary J. Blige, Keith Sweat, Gerald Levert and James J. T. Taylor. Amassing 26 gold and platinum awards, Dunn produced fitness video stars Jody Watley, Joannie Greggains, and Denise Austin's ESPN show "Getting Fit." He has also met the commercial hurdle of Madison Avenue with over a dozen commercials for McDonald's, United Airlines and the highly acclaimed SUPERBOWL 21 Wendy's "Chicken Nugget" commercial featuring Kool and The Gang.

Present-day projects include: As a first-time author writing two books; "Masculine Vulnerabilities: the POWER of an inner man revealed" and "Something About the Hour," with his publisher Hollis Media Group. He is also the Music Director and media consultant on the television pilot "Sweetheart of the Week" game show.

Dunn's extensive role in film and television production now includes the role of director. He is directing the 2018 true story "Church Girls": the seduction of religion based on the abusive culture of clergy and women in the church. The movie is an adaptation of the book. He is the host of the weekly show Men4men Better Living on Roku and producer of the Sunday Blessings empowerment 1-minute segment.

Also, Dunn became an ADVOCATE for Survivors of domestic violence with the "National Council on Domestic Abuse," after realizing the magnitude of his personal story of surviving a violent-riddle household as a teenager at the hands of his then-stepfather. When he became a FATHER, he consciously decided to end the cycle that was imposed on him and merged the experience as a teaching mantle with his music outreach to help educate young males struggling with their identity. Additionally, to undergird those who lack guidance with life skills as one of his many contributions to the next generation.

In addition to his already committed professional life, Pearson along with business partner, Dr. Janice Hollis of the Hollis Media Group in PA, created the joint-venture "Hollis Pearson Media, LLC" that launched in October 2014, which is a full-service media firm providing services in movie development, television and film scoring, arrangements, composing, media campaigns, record distribution and artist representation.

Finally, his latest music CD "The Love Suite" featuring "Classic Romance" is available nationwide.

PRODUCT PAGE

FORTHCOMING TITLE

Late Summer 2018

"SOMETHING ABOUT THE HOUR"

MUSIC

Available www.hollispearsonmedia.com

Hollis Pearson Media

RECOMMENDED SITES

www.hollispearsonmedia.com

www.men4menbetterliving.com

http://sundayblessings54.blogspot.com/

www.sujicmusic.com

PUBLIC RELATIONS

For Interviews contact Hollis Media Group

800-925-6117 or email:

Hollismediagroup@outlook.com

Join Dunn Pearson, Jr. Music, and Book Club